Texas Raid

My Experience of the 2008 Raid on the YFZ Ranch

Ammon Jeffs

This book is an account of some of my experiences in the FLDS, told to the best of my ability and recollection. Some names have been changed to protect the privacy of certain individuals.

First Edition

Contents

I dedicate this book to the memory of my dear Mother,

and to all my brothers and sisters.

Prologue

"Ammon, mother is really sick. Mother Nette says we need to hurry and be good, so we can go see her," my sister Rachel told me one morning in July 2004. Mother Annette was Mother's older sister and Father's first wife. As a fourteen-year-old, I had grown weary of trying to live perfect enough to go to "Zion", the place Father had established for the most faithful of his followers. I had been trying to be good for so long, now. "Zion" still seemed so far away to me.

A few days previous, I had gone swimming with my friends, Jim Allred's boys, up the Narrows. It was fun to have adventure again. I had been hired to work with them at the Dagrow Truss plant in Colorado City, Arizona. It was owned by two of Jim Allred's oldest sons, David and Guy. Jim Allred was Father's cousin and we did a lot with his family.

Us boys worked hard on building trusses, so we could get enough free time for adventure. I spent nearly all my time with Uncle Jim's boys now. I ate meals with them and played games with them. Now we were hiking and swimming together. I only went home once it was late in the evening. I felt ready to live life to the fullest, even if I was separated from all my siblings.

"You need to come with me right now! I'm supposed to take you home right away!" Warren Allred hollered to me as he drove into the yard of the Truss plant late that afternoon, the dust curling up behind him. Warren was our boss at work. I had called Warren earlier that day, begging him to take us up the Narrows again, because the day had been scorching hot. But he sounded different than any previous time he had come to take me home. Something was urgent. Why did I need to rush home? Was something wrong? Was this about Mother? Or was Father going to let me go to "Zion" now?

Part 1

My Early Life

Chapter One

The Early Years

I was born in April 1990, to Warren Jeffs and Barbara Barlow, his tenth child and third son. We had two mothers at the time, and I was my mother's fourth child. Mother was Father's second wife. I lived in Sandy, Utah, with my family near the mouth of Little Cottonwood Canyon for the first eight years of my life. All our family lived in one home. We were kept isolated from the outside world to a large degree.

The FLDS community in the Salt Lake City, Utah, area lived scattered across the valley. We came together for work projects, helping one another in building improvements. The members of the community worked in various businesses throughout the valley, supporting their families. All the children attended the private church school located at my Grandfather, Rulon Jeffs', property. Father's home was located next to my Grandfather's property.

I had a happy childhood and loved hiking the nearby mountains, picking berries, and playing games with my siblings and cousins. I spent all the time I could outside.

Our yard had a nice lawn, a garden, sandbox, and fruit trees planted around the house. In the back by the fence, there was a tiny forest. I loved playing "Cowboys and Indians" with my siblings back there or imagining I was a pioneer in a new land. Our property had a six-foot concrete wall along the street and the yard was fully fenced with chain link and wooden slat fences. In the summer, we worked in the garden and did jobs around the house. When our jobs were finished, we had fun playing with each other in the sandbox or swinging on the swings. In the evening, Mother would have all us kids go around the yard and make sure everything was neat and clean. We children loved going barefoot. Mother Barbara and Mother Annette told us we could only go barefoot outside during the months that didn't have an "r" in them.

Shortly after I turned two years old, I figured out how to climb the trees. I showed Mosiah how to climb also. Mosiah was six months older than me. His mother was Mother Annette. We started with the fruit trees, but soon began climbing the two large pine trees in our front yard. One day, we slipped outside and climbed to the top of one pine tree. No one could find us anywhere. We quietly sat up there, watching everyone in the family search for us. Finally, one of the girls spotted us in the treetop. Our mothers were frightened and ordered us to come down immediately. We replied, "we don't know how."

One day when I was five years old, Father took us on a hike up the "ridge" and over to the "two trees." I was meandering along, looking at the trees and watching the birds. Suddenly I realized on the trail in front of me was a pile of olives. "This is where they get olives," I thought, "olives are yum!" I stooped down and picked one up. Just as I was popping it into my mouth, Father grabbed my hand and said, "No way! Don't eat that. That's deer poop!"

I got into my share of mischief with my brother Mosiah and had plenty of spankings. One night when we were supposed to be sleeping, we decided to play like we were eggs hatching into chicks. To be white like an egg, we took off our pajamas and were in our long white underwear. We'd curl up in a ball, trying to look like an egg. Then we'd hatch by putting our pajamas back on. While we were doing this, our oldest sister Maryanne walked in our room. We played like we were asleep, but she saw us in our undies. She immediately told Father. Father gave us a long talk on how wicked it was to be uncovered like that. Then he had us go choose a stick off the pear tree for a whipping. Mosiah and I competed to find a stick that would whistle the loudest when we swung them through the air. Our whipping stung that time!

Another time, we sneaked out of bed to play in the laundry room. We heard someone coming, so we jumped into the dryer and shut the door. After a few minutes, the dryer door opened and there stood Father, visibly shaken. He told us if someone had come in and started the dryer, we would have died. To reinforce the lesson, he shut the door and played like he was turning it on. We screamed for him to let us out. We never tried that hiding place again.

"Mozy, look, there's a car by our wall," I said one summer afternoon when we were five years old. "Mozy" was my brother Mosiah, the sibling closest to my age.

"Those are wicked gentiles. They are not supposed to park by our wall," he replied.

"Should we throw rocks at them, so they'll go away?"

We carefully climbed the wall and started throwing rocks at the car. The occupants of the car had crossed the road and gone hiking up the mountain. One of my rocks crashed through the back window. That scared us and we jumped off the wall. Mosiah ran and told Father I had broken the window on a "gentile's" car, plainly forgetting his own involvement. Gentiles were anyone not part of our faith and Father had taught us they were very wicked. Father scolded me and told me I had to pay for the broken window. Mother gathered me up and walked me outside to give them a check for the damage. When we walked out the gate, the car was gone. I was immensely relieved, though I never forgot the lesson.

Mother taught me well as a child. She taught me honesty and self-denial. She taught me God was real and instilled in me the habit to pray morning and night. Mother worked hard to help keep our family fed. She did sewing jobs at home. Often, we kids helped her turn her sewing articles right side out when she finished them. Father taught in the school, which had an all-volunteer faculty. When school was out, he performed church duties for his father, Rulon Jeffs.

Mother was keen to know the needs of her children. I could always go to her room if I had a bad dream, was sad, or felt ill. She always awoke when I came to her room no matter how quiet I tried to be. Mother had the rare capacity to treat all the children in our large family equal, no matter who the mother of the child was and had no favorites. She was a woman of strong determination.

Rulon Jeffs was the head of the church at this time. Church for the FLDS community in the Salt Lake area was held in the private school located on his property. This was next door to our home. We would walk up the sidewalk to his place for Sunday School and General Meeting. We had Sunday School on Sunday morning and church every Sunday afternoon. Church was two hours long.

The largest branch of the FLDS lived in the twin cities of Hildale, Utah and Colorado City, Arizona. We called that place Short Creek. Almost everyone living in Short Creek was part of the FLDS church. The complete membership of the church was between five and six thousand members at this time. About four thousand members lived in Short Creek. The rest were in the Salt Lake Valley and Creston, British Columbia, Canada.

When I was six years old, I started school in Alta Academy, the private school owned by my Grandfather. Father was the Principal of Alta

Academy. Since the school was located on my Grandfather's property, I only had to walk up the sidewalk from our house to school next door. I loved going to school and had fun with my classmates. Reading was my favorite subject. I was an avid reader by the time I was five years old, and I read any book I could get a hold of.

In 1998, Rulon Jeffs had a stroke that greatly incapacitated him. Father took over appointments with the church members and largely took over the guidance of the church.

In September 1998, Father moved us to Short Creek in conjunction with his father's family as part of a gathering of the FLDS from the Salt Lake City area to be with the main body of the church. We were told the destruction of the wicked was about to commence and we needed to leave the Salt Lake Valley before that happened. At eight years old, I was happy to move to a new place with new adventures. The rest of the FLDS community in the Salt Lake Valley would move down to Short Creek three years later.

My life at that time was pleasant, and I enjoyed going to school, participating in all the community events, and helping to build up Short Creek. Father was the Principal of our new private school which was called Jeffs Academy. On Saturdays, I went to the communities' zoo and cleaned animal pens with my two older brothers, Levi and Mosiah. During hot summer days, we three often weeded the long rows of vegetables in the massive community garden.

We also had time for entertainments. We played games and had family programs. Singing was important to Father, and we sang every morning and evening before prayer times. Friday night, we had a family program with skits and songs. On Sunday evening, we sang songs for about one hour. These were happy times for me.

In the summer months, us three oldest boys were part of the "Marching Boys." This had been established to help the boys in the community find purpose and discipline. On practice days, we arose at 4:30 am and went to drill. We learned basic military maneuvers and learned good discipline there. We performed at all the community events and marched in the towns' parade on the 24th of July. The 24th was Pioneer Day in Utah, which we celebrated as the day Brigham Young, leader of the LDS church entered the Salt Lake Valley for the first time and designated it as the new gathering place for the members of The Church of Jesus Christ of Latter-Day Saints.

The next four years passed mostly uneventful for me. I went to school each year. My summers were spent at home most of the time. I worked and played with my many siblings. My two older brothers, Levi and Mosiah, and I often went up to my grandfather's property next door and did garden and yard work for him. I had many additional siblings born into the family. It became normal to us kids to have three or four children born into our family each year.

After I turned twelve in the spring of 2002, I began working with my cousins, Uncle Leroy's boys, on construction projects around the community. We generally did framing and flooring projects. Our work was donated to the United Effort Plan trust, and we received no pay. The United Effort Plan trust was set up by leaders of the Short Creek community in 1942. It originally consisted of several large parcels of land which were donated to the trust by faithful members of the group. All

FLDS members in Short Creek lived and built their homes on the land owned by the UEP trust, which was controlled by the church leadership.

Early that summer, Father allowed us to go on a three-day camping trip with Uncle Leroy's sons. We went up Cedar Mountain to Navajo Lake and found a spring on the back of the lake where there were large schools of fish. We caught an abundance of trout, and I was hooked on fishing for life.

Chapter Two

Mother, Why are You Here?

A t the end of July 2002, Father's and Grandfather's family went on a camping trip together at Yankee Meadows in the mountains northeast of Parowan, Utah. It was the first time I could remember going camping with my grandfather. He was 92 years old and quite frail, so he slept in a motorhome that had been provided for him. The rest of us slept in tents. We had a great time fishing, hiking, horse-riding, and mountain biking.

On September 8, 2002, my paternal grandfather, Rulon Jeffs passed away. Father had consistently taught us that Grandfather would be completely renewed with his body restored to youthful vigor. He told us Grandfather would be the last "prophet" who would lead us through the judgements of God on the wicked and establish "Zion" on this continent. When Grandfather died, Father told us he was now "renewed."

After Grandfather's passing, Father took over the leadership of the church. He rapidly changed many things in the FLDS community. Father had 25 wives before he took over the church leadership. He subsequently married many of his father's wives. Grandfather had approximately 60 wives when he died, most of whom were young women and had recently been married to him within the last few years of his life.

We called all the women married to Father our "mothers." Each one was referred to as "Mother (first name)."

Father isolated himself from the church membership and often his family, claiming we were treating him and his teachings lightly. He said God was requiring him to stay away from us. He also began to isolate his wives and children from the rest of the church membership. The government pressure from the states of Utah and Arizona was growing because of underage marriages he had been performing. He felt like he and his family were in great danger of a government raid. He often told us there were apostates seeking to harm us and take our lives.

In 2003, he had the members of the church build a tall brick wall all the way around our property, which we called the "Jeffs block." It consisted of a city block in Hildale, UT. Father, Uncle Nephi, Uncle Seth, Uncle Isaac, Rich Allred, and Nathaniel Allred all lived there with their families. There were two massive houses and five smaller houses on the "block." By mid-2003, Father suppressed all community celebrations. He even stopped our church meetings and all religious ordinances among the people, although he continued performing marriages.

My mother learned she had breast cancer in the winter of 2003. By spring, she began chemotherapy treatments. This made her ill most of the time. Father began to be gone all the time and kept secret what he was doing. I would later learn he was searching out and purchasing properties where he could start new communities in preparation for his abandonment of Short Creek. They would be "places of refuge" where he could hide from the coming government pressure.

Mother began to research natural remedies for cancer and found several cures she felt would work for her. She let me read all the online research she did, and I was supportive of her finding this natural cure. Around the time we started school in October of 2003, Father told mother, against her wishes, that the Lord required that she go through chemotherapy again. I was distraught when Mother told me she was getting chemo again and protested with her until she informed me that Father was requiring this of her.

In the fall of 2003, Father pulled all his children out of Jeffs Academy and had us do home school. I skipped eighth grade and started high school with three of my older siblings. I was very involved in my schoolwork. When school was out, us boys milked two cows and cared for our small flock of chickens and turkeys. I loved any sports we were allowed and spent any free time I had after school practicing rollerblading, basketball, free space, (a game like capture the flag, with a "free space" behind enemy lines) dare base, and many other games.

Members of our family started disappearing in mid-2003. Father's youngest underage wives were gone. A few of my youngest siblings and their mothers also disappeared. I realized Father had something going on and must have another house elsewhere that he was keeping secret.

On November 29, 2003, I noticed Mother gathering and packing the belongings of her three youngest children. I asked her what was happening, and she refused to answer. I realized all the mothers were secretly packing up the belongings of most of my younger siblings. At dinner that night I asked Father if there was something he needed to tell us, but he would say nothing. Afterwards, when we went outside to play, he called my older brother Levi aside and told him to pack his belongings as discreetly as possible.

I was the president of one of the deacon quorums. (A quorum consisting of twelve individuals who had been ordained to the office of deacon in the Aaronic Priesthood) I had a president's meeting I had to attend that night. On my way out of the house, I noticed a trailer being loaded by several of Father's assistants. This left me puzzled. "If Father's taking all the children away, why won't he tell me?" I wondered. When I returned at 8:30 that night, it was unusually dark around the Jeffs block, and no one answered the bell on the gate. I climbed over the tall brick wall at the top of the property and ran down to our house. The lights were out, and it was dead silent inside. I peered in a couple of the children's rooms and realized nearly all my younger siblings were gone, so I rushed upstairs to Mother's room and found her on the couch weeping. I asked, "Mother, why are you here?" She replied, "Father had you and Josephine stay because he said the 'place' wouldn't be Zion if you went there."

She told me the Lord had not given Father her name to go "Zion" either. Mother's two oldest, Rachel and Melanie were married and lived with their husbands. Levi, age 15, Jacob, age 6, Joseph, age 4, and Amber, age 2, were gone. Josephine, age 10 and me, age 13, remained with her. I was deeply saddened and cried myself to sleep that night.

This dealt a severe blow to Mother's health. When Father told her he was going to take her three youngest children along with her oldest son to a secret place without her, she remonstrated and told him due to her cancer, she could die soon and would never see her children again. The doctors had given her only a few months to live. He insisted he was doing God's will. He claimed God had shown him her children were in great danger and her support was needed for their protection, convincing her to participate. When the children were taken to the vehicles they were departing in, he required her to cheerfully hand her children to him so they would believe she supported him in taking them from her.

The next morning Father called and told mother to talk in Sunday School. She stated that her children being separated from her and taken to an unknown location was the same as if they were dead. She was heartbroken over this. No biological mothers were allowed to accompany their children when Father took them. Approximately 20 of my siblings were taken away that night.

A few days later, Father called Mother Annette and told her the 10 of his unmarried children that had remained must be taken from the Jeffs block and live in other homes around Short Creek in utmost secrecy. He claimed the Lord had shown him that his children would be destroyed if he didn't remove them all from the Jeffs block. We were to leave the property without letting Mother know. While the family was eating dinner that night, we slipped away with Mother Annette and were taken to live at James Allred's home across town. When Mother discovered our absence, she broke down and wept again.

After three weeks, Father returned from "Zion" to Short Creek and brought Mother over to visit us. He gave her permission to secretly check on us every few days. At the same time, Mother started her second round of chemotherapy treatments and became very ill.

"Zion" now became a place in our minds that Father was gathering the most faithful and obedient people of the church to. The location was secret. Father told us only those the Lord named personally to him could gather there or know anything about it.

We called James Allred "Uncle Jim." While we were living at Uncle Jim's, Father had us keep our presence secret. Uncle Jim bought privacy vinyl slats for his chain link fence so we could work and play outside. If anyone came over, we had to run to our rooms and hide until they left.

Changes were constantly happening, and soon, most of my siblings that had initially remained in Short Creek were also taken to live in "Zion."

When Mother Annette left for "Zion," Father had Mother come live with us at Uncle Jim's.

In February 2004, Mosiah, Leroy, Josephine, Mother Barbara, Mother Shannon, and I moved to Uncle Leroy Jeffs' home. In March, Josephine went to "Zion" and only I remained with Mother. Mother was sad and lonely without her children around. She longed after them constantly. They sometimes sent tape recordings to her of them singing or learning how to read. She was rarely allowed to speak to them on the phone. I could see it taking a terrible toll on her health.

One day when I had a dental appointment in St George, Mother and I saw a newspaper headline that reported the discovery of the FLDS building a compound near Eldorado, Texas. Later that day, Father called all his family in Short Creek and stressed the importance of never looking at the newspaper to discover what the Lord was having him do. Afterwards, Mother spoke to him and confessed what we had seen about his place in Texas. He had her call me aside, tell me we had done wrong, and swear me to secrecy about it.

In April 2004, Father moved us back to the "Jeffs block." My sisters Rachel and Melanie both lived there with their husbands.

Father brought Jacob and Amber to live with Mother in mid-April. They had not been as obedient as Father required while they were in "Zion." Jacob only stayed in Short Creek for a short time before Father took him back to "Zion."

As Mother's condition worsened, she developed pneumonia and required oxygen all the time. When this happened, Father called and talked to a few of us in Mother's room on speakerphone. He told everyone to exert great faith and never allow the slightest doubt to enter their minds about her full recovery. He then had me take the phone to my room and speak to him privately. He informed me as mother's condition worsened, her suffering would become more intense and hinted that she was going to die. I was heartbroken.

In the first of June 2004, Father called me and said he was going to take Mother and Amber to "Zion." I would have to stay because I was not good enough to go yet. He told me to arise the next morning at 4 am and help Mother pack her belongings into the vehicle she would be traveling in. I was very sad and cried myself to sleep that night. The next morning, I awoke at 6 am. I discovered I had set my alarm to 4 pm instead of am. I ran to Mother's room, sure that she would have awoken me, but she was gone. I sank onto her couch, devastated.

After Mother left, I was allowed a telephone conversation with her twice for a couple of minutes each time. Both times Father cut our conversation short. She never told me her health condition and I eagerly hoped she was beginning to recover.

Chapter Three

R17: A Place of Refuge

I n May 2004, at age 14, I started working at the Dagrow Truss plant, an FLDS owned business, with my brother Mosiah and Uncle Jim Allred's boys building wooden roof trusses. We worked without pay most of the time. I was glad to have work to keep my mind busy so I wouldn't feel sad about my circumstances.

On the morning of July 7, after I went to work, my sister Rachel called me on Warren Allred's cell phone. She told me Mother Annette had called and told her that we needed to be good so we could go to "Zion" and be with Mother. Mother's health was failing fast. I felt anxiety building in me and hoped mother wouldn't die before I could reunite with her. It was a hot, dusty day in Short Creek. All of us boys wanted to go up the "Narrows," a beautiful canyon northeast of town, to go swimming. Late that afternoon, Warren Allred came driving into the Dagrow Truss yard in his old green Chevy truck and called out to me to jump in immediately. He was supposed to hurry me home. He left Mosiah there with his brothers.

I hastily joined Warren, who rushed me home to meet Uncle Isaac. He informed me that Mother was gravely ill and hospitalized in San Angelo, Texas. Father wanted her remaining children in Short Creek to visit her one last time. He instructed me to gather a bag of clothes and head to Roy Allred's place, my brother-in-law, who had a vehicle ready for our trip to see my mother.

I held onto the hope that this journey might lead me to move to "Zion," where most of my siblings lived. Being apart from them for seven months was agonizing. I longed to reunite and live together as a family once again.

After an hour's wait, Rachel, Melanie, and I joined Roy Allred and Uncle Isaac. We embarked on an overnight seventeen-hour drive. Rachel and I sat in the back seat of the Ford Excursion we were traveling in. Rachel was seven months pregnant and seemed uncomfortable the whole time. I kept good track of our route so I would know the way to "Zion."

We arrived at the Shannon Medical Center in San Angelo, TX around 11 am the next morning. Upon our arrival, we were quickly ushered into my mother's room. I was shocked to witness her deteriorating health; it was evident that she was close to death. She looked as if she had aged ten years in the six weeks since she had left Short Creek. She was pleased to see us but expressed a strong desire to leave the hospital and be at home with her family before her passing.

While we were there, the hospital released her, and we brought her to the hotel room we had prepared. She lost consciousness when attempting to walk in and was in critical condition while there. I was filled with fear that she might pass away while we stayed in the hotel. When she regained consciousness, she pleaded to return home immediately.

Father called and informed us individually that our mother was not going to survive. Heartbreakingly, he instructed me to return to Short Creek because the Lord hadn't told him I could live in the Texas community, leaving me deeply saddened.

Mother was taken back to the community near Eldorado, while Rachel and I were not permitted to accompany her. Roy Allred and Melanie quietly disappeared that afternoon, Father allowing them to go to the ranch to be with mother. That night, I stayed in a hotel room with Rachel, barely able to get any sleep.

The following morning, Rachel and I set out for Short Creek with Uncle Isaac. I expected to get word any moment of Mother's passing. I felt desolate, and my life felt shattered. We traveled for 9 hours without hearing anything.

When we reached Albuquerque, New Mexico, Father called and announced that the Lord had named Rachel and I as worthy participants in the "mission" he was establishing. Consequently, we were allowed to go to the new community in Texas. I was overjoyed to finally be allowed to move to the "Zion" I had been hoping to go to for so long. As we traveled back, we underwent extensive preparation training, which consisted of listening to hours of recorded teachings by Father about why he was establishing these communities. He required us to enter a covenant to live with all things in common and support him in doing this work of building "Zion." He told us he was building several "places of refuge" for the gathering of the saints. Hastily turning back, we arrived in Texas around 11:00 pm.

Mother learned we were coming several hours before our arrival and kept speaking of us to the family around her until she became unconscious. This was the condition we found her in when we arrived. We stayed by her side, tenderly speaking to her of our love for her until she passed away around 5:30 am. I was devastated to lose my mother and overwhelmed by the rapid changes occurring in my life. I was only fourteen years old at this time. Thus began my new life in the FLDS Texas community, known as R17.

Mother's funeral and burial took place swiftly because Father was paranoid about government officials or dissidents from our religion knowing his location. Immediately after the funeral, he had me report to Ernest Jessop, who oversaw the construction crews. I was put on the workforce with the other men.

I moved into the boy's room in the home that had recently been built for Father's family. The home was crowded. At night, family members were sleeping anywhere they could find a space. I quickly learned that my interaction with the family would be minimal. I could sleep at home but was to be up at 5:00 am and to men's prayer by 6:00 am with all the workers. After prayer the crews ate breakfast together and went right to work. I almost never saw my siblings.

I learned the profound meaning of hard work and sleep deprivation. A new community was being built on a former hunting ranch in the middle of the desert in the western Texas hill country. There were many ongoing construction projects with tight deadlines that Father had set: a massive log home for Father, a smaller house for the members of the First Presidency, a large log Storehouse, stonework on the Meeting House, and excavation for the Temple's foundation.

Our workdays commenced after 6:00 am men's prayer and breakfast, extending until 2:00 am the next morning. We broke for a prayer time and lunch at noon. We also had a prayer time and dinner at 8:00 pm. I ate all my meals with the workers. A few of Father's childless wives made meals for all the workers. Two weeks after my arrival, our morning prayer time was changed to 5:00 am. All this was a monumental change for me, yet I embraced the learning and challenges with enthusiasm. I swiftly acquired numerous building skills, expanding my expertise to encompass framing, electrical, drywall, roofing, painting, plumbing, finish work, heavy equipment operation, stone cutting, concrete, woodwork, and gardening.

Shortly after my arrival, Uncle Merril Jessop was appointed to be our bishop, overseeing the community and ranch. He became a fatherly figure to me, imparting valuable life lessons. I devoted myself to our "mission," finding happiness and busyness within it. My interactions with my father were infrequent, and my work primarily involved building log homes and assisting in the construction of the temple. There were numerous occasions when I worked for 36 to 72 hours without sleep, often competing with other teenage boys to see who could endure the longest. I often wondered if I'd ever know what it was like not to feel exhausted.

My longest stretch of continuous work was 76 hours in September 2004. We aimed to construct three 7,000-square-foot homes within a month, and I was determined to contribute without a break. However, upon reaching the 72-hour mark, exhaustion clouded my thoughts, and by 6:00 am on the fourth morning, I could hardly function. There was no energy left in my hands and no mental capacity. I collapsed on my bed around 10:00 pm and slept for a straight 16 hours.

In June 2005, I pushed myself for 48 hours, slept 2 hours, then endured another 42 hours before collapsing while working. Father found me at 6 am after I had been sleeping for 6 hours and had me promise I would go until midnight before I would retire for anymore rest.

Despite our intense workload, we young fellows found moments for fun and mischief, albeit quite different from typical teenage activities. Our fun included engaging in activities like burning construction waste, racing on four-wheelers, playing tag on the log walls of homes we were erecting, and igniting gasoline to create towering flames. However, this brought me some trouble with the bishop and his counselors, who forbade us from playing with fire. We enjoyed having steak cookouts out in the bushes, but Father severely reprimanded us when he learned of it and had us cease. Father would occasionally call one of the phones on the ranch and check on me. He always asked me if any teenage boys and I were having immoral conversations together. This meant he was wondering if we were talking about girls which was something all FLDS boys were forbidden to do. I often wondered why he asked this. We were constantly busy and exhausted. We were trying to be perfectly obedient to his intense religious teachings. Not being strictly obedient meant we would be sent away. Talking about girls was the furthest thing from our minds at the time.

There were occasions when I served on security duty, driving around the ranch on a four-wheeler, checking the fence line, roaming the back roads, and chasing the deer. I detested being stationed in the tiny structure known as "the doghouse" or "tower" which was located atop the concrete powder silo near the north fence line. However, it did offer some opportunities for much-needed sleep. Gate watch, a more comfortable option, allowed for easier rest but was usually designated for older men. An eight-foot fence had been erected around the entire property before Father purchased the land. We had a one-mile easement between two of our neighbor's properties. We had to go through two gates to enter or leave the ranch. Our security role aimed solely to deter intruders and never to spy on or coerce the residents.

One morning when on tower duty, I sank into a deep sleep. I was suddenly aroused by the noise of the radio; everyone on security was trying to awaken me. Suddenly Father's voice came over the radio, asking the watchman on the tower if there were any airplanes flying around. I drowsily stepped out of the doghouse, stretched, and looked around in the sky. Then I saw Father at the base of the tower, watching me. He was showing Wayne Fischer around the property. Father had just married Wayne's twelve-year-old daughter and was patronizing him. I was embarrassed to be caught sleeping.

Father was afraid outsiders would become curious and try sneaking on the property to see what he was having us do there. We caught migrants from Mexico a few times. There was only one time I recall an intruder sneaking on the ranch. He tried to sneak on the temple lot, but the man on tower saw him and called for help. All the workers scoured the land, searching for the intruder, but he escaped.

During scorching summer days, some of us would sneak up to the gravel pit ponds for a quick swim at lunchtime. Those were the only self-taught swimming lessons I ever had. It was frowned upon by our leaders but largely conducted under the radar.

When school resumed in the fall of 2004, I inquired of Father about continuing my studies, but he instructed me to focus on the construction projects instead. I had skipped eighth grade and commenced high school a year earlier, at the age of 13, but could only complete one quarter before the drastic changes disrupted my education.

Whenever we missed a deadline, Father would strongly rebuke us and tell us this was because of a lack of obedience and faithfulness on our part. He would claim God was about to scourge or destroy us because of our disobedience and complacency. Then he would inform us he had pled with God to spare our lives and offered to atone for our sins so God wouldn't destroy us. Father "atoned" for us often. This atoning was purportedly like the atonement of Jesus on the cross and in the Garden of Gethsemane, although of lesser degree.

The occasion that stood out in my young mind the strongest was in August 2004. We had missed the 10-day deadline for the sidewalks around Father's house and the Meeting House. The deadline also included the completion of the storehouse, concrete shoe shelves built around the Meeting House entries, and the stonework on the east end of the Meeting House. Father sent two of the leading elders, Ernest Jessop and Allen Steed, away. Then he held a long meeting with us, rebuking us for our "sins." At the end of the meeting, he said a long prayer. In sorrowful tones, he called upon God to remember the martyrdom of each of the "prophets." He mentioned each one by name. By the time he said, "And remember the martyrdom of your servant Rulon Jeffs," he acted like he could scarcely speak. He was crouched down, leaning heavily upon the lectern, acting like he was suffering extreme pain for us. After pausing for a moment, he said, "Thank you, Father," in slow, painful tones. Then he closed the prayer. At that moment, he collapsed onto the floor. Many in the congregation were weeping. Mother Naomie walked to the front of the room and told everyone to leave. We all departed, greatly humbled and repentant. I thought Father was dying and was very scared. Later, he told us he was atoning for our sins and disobedience, so God could give us another chance. He often told me he had bought me with a price. He was claiming he had atoned for me, otherwise God would have destroyed me or cast me off forever.

From July to December 2004, we built eight log homes and one storehouse. The footings for the temple had been excavated out of solid rock and poured with concrete. We had also cut trenches and run underground power to all the homes and lots in the community. A large stone quarry was being excavated by operators on several rock saws for the stone on that would be used on the temple. A saw yard for stone-cutting had been built close to the temple site. R17 was a flurry of activity.

In December, we were tasked with cutting stone for the temple's foundation walls. It was impossible to achieve by month-end. Despite our diligent efforts in the stone-cutting yard that month, we fell far short of the required deadline Father had set for all the stone blocks to be cut. Consequently, he had us switch to pouring concrete walls. We continued to fall short on the deadlines Father would set. We missed the deadline for the foundation walls and the exterior framing and drying in of the temple. The entire workforce was involved in trying to meet these deadlines. This was the most demanding period on the ranch, leaving little time for anything beyond work. My life could be summed up in intense schedules and minimal sleep during the first six months of 2005. Father had Uncle Merril enforce what he expected our workloads to be. Uncle Merril was required to report often in detail to Father about the ongoing projects and the obedience and diligence of the men.

Once the exterior framing of the temple was complete, I returned to the saw yard to assist in the stone cutting. In April 2005, I was relocated to work on the temple's interior as we strove to meet Father's deadline for the temple's completion. Initially allotted only 2 hours of sleep, Father eventually increased it to 4 hours for us teenage boys. There were instances where we'd go days without sleep.

Our motto when building the temple was, "The best we can do is barely good enough for God." Despite the tight deadlines, we aimed to make our handiwork beautiful. We had approximately 75 men working on the temple project. This included workers in three woodshops building all the trims, doors, cabinets, and furniture; and the stone cutting crew in the saw yard.

When I moved from stone cutting to the interior of the temple, I was put on the drywall crew. We hung sheetrock for hours on end. This was an intense workout for me. When sheetrock was complete, I was transferred to the flooring crew. I laid a large amount of carpet and tile and became apt at that trade.

We were required to have 28 men always working in the temple: seven on each floor. We struggled to maintain that ratio but did our best. Father required us to wait for another workman to trade us off before we could get our two hours of sleep. Sometimes we were kept up much longer than 24 hours waiting for a tradeoff. Some of the men cracked under the pressure and became angry when no one came to relieve them at the end of their shift. I often stayed up longer than my shift to allow my coworkers to get much-needed rest.

Father forbade any complaining among the men, telling us if we murmured, God would be angry and withdraw the blessings of heaven. He held a meeting with us one afternoon, informing us God was offended with many of the workers for allowing themselves to have a silent complaint in their minds about the workload and their utter exhaustion. "If you start going down," he said, "go down on your knees and pray for the strength of heaven. Then arise and keep going." All of us were dedicated to the mission and strove to obey.

When we missed the June 12 completion deadline for the temple, I slept for 12 hours straight and awoke to excruciating growing pains. I hadn't slept like that for many months. For the next few nights, I also slept for 12 hours, because of my utter exhaustion from the previous months' work. When Father learned of this, he again instructed me to limit my sleep to 4 hours.

Once the interior work was completed, our schedule became less stringent, allowing everyone to get 5 hours of sleep each night. In July, I returned to the stone-cutting yard and worked there until the stonework was finished in mid-December. I became skilled in operating a 6-foot-blade radial rock saw.

My coworkers and I often played pranks on each other to alleviate the monotony of our tasks. We had constructed shelters on our saws to protect us from the weather. Sometimes, we would sneak up behind a coworker's shelter and shake it violently if they had fallen asleep. On other occasions, if someone dozed off in the skid steer after using it, we'd use the forklift to hoist it off the ground, leaving them hanging. We had firehoses for washing the sludge the stone cutting produced, but at times, we used them for water fights. We had a pond in the saw yard where our wastewater was collected, and some of us younger boys wanted to introduce frogs into it. On a rainy day, my friend Patrick Dutson and I gathered mating toads from the wash, stuffed our pockets with them, and released them into the pond.

We acquired a 135-foot lattice boom crane for heavy lifting on the temple. To counter the passive nature of working in the saw yard, I got the other teenage boys into climbing to the top of the crane where we would relish the beautiful morning sunrises over the plains. Sometimes, we would sneak up there during our lunch break and dare each other to get on the very top. One morning several of the boys climbed the crane during work hours and began showing off and waving to the men on the ground. They were noticed by many members of the community who reported them to the bishop. The boys who were involved were publicly corrected by Uncle Merril as an example of deviating from their responsibilities. This was spoken about at our prayer times for the next two weeks. Thankfully, I had slept in until 7 that morning and escaped the public scolding, although I was reprimanded for arising so late. Uncle Merril was still kind to the boys and told them he would have done likewise when he was their age. But Father expected him to keep us in line.

When school commenced that year, the boys my age started attending. My coworkers in the saw yard approached me, expressing their willingness to endure any punishment necessary to prevent me from attending school and continuing to operate the rock saw. I appreciated their acknowledgement of my usefulness, but hoped I could get more education. When I spoke with Father about going to school, he emphasized that my work held more significance than formal schooling, so I didn't attend that year. Other boys who did go to school were withdrawn in the second quarter to pick rocks in the fields, failing to complete any curriculum for the year.

By the beginning of 2006, after the temple's completion, our work schedule eased, and boys under 18 were required to work from 6:00 am until 11:00 pm. Despite several ongoing projects, there were no fixed deadlines. During this period, Father was a fugitive from justice and was on the FBI's ten most wanted list. He was avoiding arrest in the states of

Utah and Arizona. We were kept in the dark about the details of the cases against him. All we knew was the government and "apostates" were after him, trying to stop the work of God. When he came to the ranch, we were instructed never to disclose his whereabouts. Although he occasionally stayed at the ranch, we seldom saw him. Often, he came without our knowledge. He would ride around the land in the backseat of a truck or SUV, checking on the various projects. He spent a lot of time traveling around the United States. His whereabouts were extremely secret. When he was at the ranch, he would occasionally visit with his family and come to a meal or give religious teachings to us.

He recorded sermons for the people on the land to listen to each Sabbath. We had four hours of recorded trainings he required us to listen to each Sunday, week after week.

In July 2006, Father came to the ranch and spent more time with the people. He would have the bishop gather families in small groups to his home, where he would give them religious teachings. He also began arranging for the start of the next school year.

Father was always invested in the school and appointed all teachers and assistants of each class. Because Father was arranging for the start of school, I again asked him if I could attend high school. He inquired if I was sure I complete my schoolwork if he allowed me to attend. I promised him I would. I had gone over two and one-half years without any schooling and desperately wanted more education.

Just before school started, on August 28, 2006, Father was apprehended by the law in Nevada and put in jail. Learning about his arrest left me deeply saddened and angry. I had been taught his innocence and believed he was being persecuted for doing God's will. His arrest disrupted the mission we were engaged in and brought the church to a standstill. I was replacing carpet in a classroom at the school when I learned of his arrest. A dull, sickening feeling seemed to permeate everywhere on the ranch. Little did I realize the implications this would bring upon the church. Everything slowed down for several months. It never crossed my mind that he would remain in prison for life. Convinced of his innocence, we prayed incessantly for his release.

School began on September 1st. I was happy to resume my education. We called our school "Zion Academy." School was held in the meeting house we had built. The meeting house had been designed for dual use as a place to hold both church and school.

Life at R17 continued somewhat normally and we persevered with our projects. My age group of boys were expected to bear adult responsibilities, just as it had been from the time I arrived. It was challenging for the other men to accept our pursuit of education, so we skipped the first quarter and started schooling in the second quarter.

We realized how great an opportunity it was to receive further education, so we made the most of our time in school. After school hours, at 1:00 pm, we were still required to work until 6:00 pm before being able to tackle our homework.

In late January 2007, when I was 16 years old, Father called from the Purgatory Jail in Washington County, Utah, telling us he was the most wicked man on earth. He stated he was no longer the Prophet, and we should look to William E. Timpson as the true prophet. William Timpson was the current bishop of Short Creek. Father said he hoped to meet us before the judgement day, or the end of the world, and ask our forgiveness for all his wrongs. Then he hung up. We were stunned. I was raised believing he spoke for God and automatically believed him. I went to work that afternoon, wondering what was going to happen now. Would our family be broken up and spread to other families? Was the "mission" going to endure on the "places of refuge" or would we all go back to Short Creek? What family was Uncle Will going to put me in? I was very worried.

That evening, Father called several times and spoke to Uncle Merril and others, and I began hoping it wasn't true after all. I sat on the floor against the wall by the living room door with my brother Abraham, hoping Father would speak to us again. Abraham asked me when I thought Uncle Will was going to come. I told him we needed to wait and find out what Father was saying. Shortly afterward, Uncle Merril came to the living room and talked to Father's family. He told us Father was very ill and we needed to pray for him. He affirmed to us that Father was still the prophet. We were immensely relieved. Now we knew this was just one of the great tests Father told us we would undergo to see if we would stay true to him.

Father called back about ten days later and told us this was a test. God had told him to carry on as the leader of the church. A week or two later, he slipped into deep depression and recanted several times. This was kept secret from us, and we did not hear from him again until April. By then, he was ready to continue as the church leader and began to control the church and "lands of refuge" again. He required everyone on the lands of refuge to be baptized into the United Order for the first time. The United Order was an establishment within the church where we had all things in common. The United Order, also known as the law of consecration, was designed to eliminate poverty and make everyone in the community equal.

Following a year of high school, we continued our dedication to the construction projects assigned to us. In the summer of 2007, I resumed work on rock sawing as we constructed the Printing Building adjacent to the temple block. Despite Father being in jail, he maintained strict control, directing additional building projects, and setting deadlines for their completion. Father used the bishops of the various communities to carry out his requirements. After finishing the Printing Building, we were eager to pursue another year of high school. I asked Father, and to my joy, he allowed it, although we had to skip the first quarter due to completion deadlines he set on three log houses, each spanning 10,000 square feet.

Once we started school, we were given more time in the day to finish our homework than the previous year. I thoroughly enjoyed my high school classes, cherishing my teachers and striving to excel to maintain a 4.0 GPA. After school, I often went out in the bushes or on the rock piles by the temple rock quarry to complete my homework. School provided a welcome respite from the constant manual labor we were accustomed to. It made me feel my age, doing things a conventional teenage boy would do. It just felt right.

Part 2

The Raid

Chapter Four

Enemies at the Gate

Day 1

On the bright and beautiful morning of April 3, 2008, no foreboding loomed over our community. The men were engrossed in various projects—constructing a new log home, adding to the oldest duplex, excavating the sewer lagoons, and other ongoing tasks. Meanwhile, we children attended our usual school routine. After school, I completed my Geometry, Accounting, and First-Aid homework.

At 4:30 pm, a few high school boys, including Mitchel Jeffs, Leslie Steed, and I, gathered at the Tannery to discuss the English speeches we were preparing to deliver the next day. Though giving speeches was uncharted territory, we aimed to impress our English teacher and make her proud.

At 5:00 pm, Leroy Steed called his son Leslie to alert him about law enforcement officers at the gate. This caused alarm and we assembled at our homes for a prayer with our families. I was completely bewildered about why law enforcement were here. We had ongoing problems with the Texas Commission on Environmental Quality pertaining to proper environmental care and obtaining sewer lagoon permits, but nothing more than that. I hastened home, meeting my brother Levi, and we gathered with our family to pray for the Lord's protection over us. Afterward, we gathered in the dining room and attempted dinner. But none of us felt much like eating.

Increasingly curious about the situation, I felt no inclination to wait at home. Thinking there were only a few officers at the gate, I fetched a small pair of binoculars, dashed over to the grain elevator about a quarter mile south of home, and ascended to the top. Luke Jessop had just climbed up there as well, and together, we scanned the area through our binoculars. The sight that unfolded before my eyes was startling.

Gazing south toward the main gate into the community, I saw state trooper cars, ranger cars, and game warden trucks lining the county road. At Floyd West's property, two state trooper cars blocked the south gas-road gate where an old gas pipeline and accompanying maintenance road went from north to south through the ranch. Looking north toward Lynn Griffin's property, an even more surprising sight met my eyes—a SWAT (Special Weapons and Tactics) team with an armored personnel carrier (which we thought was a military tank) and weapons carrier provided by Midland County, along with several state trooper cars, barricaded the other gas-road gate. All access points were sealed, and we found ourselves surrounded by an array of law enforcement vehicles and officers.

After surveying the scene in wonder for a few minutes, I slid down the electrical conduit alongside the grain elevator, went to Uncle Merril's, borrowed Mitchel's camera, and promptly returned to the grain elevator's top to photograph the officers' positions. By then, the sun had set, and darkness began to envelop us. I descended and headed to Uncle Merril's front yard, where my friends had gathered. I shared what I'd seen. All of us had the same puzzled expression. We were unable to grasp the gravity of the situation unfolding around us. As we stood, a buzzing sound overhead caught our attention—the officers had deployed a drone to patrol the ranch.

Moments later, Richard Barlow arrived in his truck, seeking our help in preparing classrooms in the Meeting House for a government agency's imminent interviews. Bewildered, we rushed to assist, clearing out and reorganizing five upstairs classrooms by relocating desks and removing pictures of Father and other church leaders, stowing them within the grand piano in the meeting hall. Curious, I asked the school principal what was going on. He told me Child Protective Services were coming in to interview some of the teenage girls. I asked him what CPS were like, to which he grimly responded, "They're not good."

As dusk settled, we returned home and turned off all lights. We also instructed other houses to follow suit. After dressing in dark clothes, several boys, including myself, remained outside around our house, determined not to retire for the night. With the ongoing excitement, sleep was out of question.

At 9:00 pm, CPS arrived escorted by two SWAT teams, Sheriff David Doran, Ranger Brooks Long, and several state troopers and Texas Rangers. Shortly after, Uncle Merril drove up in his truck with his daughters, whom he brought for interviews. Others, like Leroy Steed, a counselor to the bishop, also arrived with their daughters. I naively hoped whatever the problem was would be resolved by morning without any issues.

An hour passed, and my uncertainty about CPS's purpose urged me to investigate further. Mitchel was nearby, so I persuaded him to accompany me. We approached the window on the school's Northwest corner, devoid of officers. I balanced on his sturdier shoulders and pressed my ear against the window. Faint voices emanated from within; unfortunately, I couldn't discern the conversation.

Exploring the North side, we found an extension ladder leading to the roof. Setting it up against the adjacent window, I secured Mitchel's digital camera and cautiously ascended. Peering through a slightly open blind, I observed Rebecca Baxter, a CPS worker, interrogating Sarabelle Steed. I discreetly captured videos and photos for a few minutes before climbing down. I hurried home to download the visuals and apprise my worried family of the situation.

Returning to the school, I discovered my friends peering through the same window. Rich Jessop, one of Uncle Merril's older sons who had been accompanying law enforcement since their arrival, intervened, warning them against upsetting the state officials. They disbanded and removed the ladder. However, undeterred, Mitchel and I fetched new batteries for the camera from the storehouse and restored the ladder. We observed Sylvia Steed being questioned before they vacated the room. Seeing the officers coming, we hurriedly removed the ladder.

Day 2

Seeking new distractions, I walked along the wall encircling the Meeting House's east end with my friends. We noticed the High School girls' classroom brightly lit with open blinds. Stealthily approaching, I witnessed Angie Voss, Tina Martinez, and several other CPS officials rifling through desks and reading girls' journals, seemingly unaware of the open blinds. As the night wore on until dawn, they continued their investigation. I returned several times until 4:00 am, capturing pictures of their activities.

Around 1:30 am, I headed to the south side of the school where the SWAT teams and a few other officers and Texas Rangers were stationed. Louis Jessop and I engaged in conversation with them. One man named Brooks Long boasted to Louis that he could summon an additional 2,000 law enforcement officers within a few hours if we created any trouble. Another officer from the Fort Stockton area chatted with us about the weather in his region and expressed his wish for us kids to get some sleep.

By 2:00 am, I returned to the north side of the building and discovered another classroom in the basement with partially open blinds. Lying on the sidewalk, I could glimpse Ruby Gutierrez, a CPS worker, and a colleague questioning Leah Jeffs. I captured a moment on video with Mitchel's camera until a nearby boy whispered, "Get up! Somebody's right there!" I quickly stood up and innocently walked away. Shortly after, an officer turned the corner to check on us. They continued questioning Leah Jeffs in that room until 4:20 am. The CPS officials kept many of these girls up all night for interrogation.

At 4:00 am, some of our men who had stayed in the school requested blankets and sleeping bags for the detained girls. CPS insisted on holding them and refused to let them go home. We gathered blankets, sleeping bags, and a box of grapes. We offered the officers grapes and food, but they declined, claiming they had provisions for at least three days located nearby. This realization unsettled me as it indicated they might stay longer than anticipated. Around 4:45 am, a cold front blew through, bringing a noticeable chill.

By 5:30 am, I ate a breakfast of cold mush. I then took a brief hour-long nap in Seth Allred's SUV while he drove around the perimeter of the ranch. Afterward, I returned home, had a quick shower, and went back to the school to observe CPS and law enforcement activities. Inside, I spoke to Leroy Steed, where I learned about the cause for the state's intervention—a prank call claiming to be Sarah Jessop Barlow alleging abuse by Dale Barlow. Dale Barlow was living in Colorado City, AZ and had previously been convicted for having an underage wife in the state of Arizona. None fitting those descriptions lived in our community. Leroy mentioned, "It's hard to find someone who doesn't exist and harder to prove that they don't." Naively, I believed proving their absence would resolve the situation, but I was wrong.

That morning, Uncle Merril requested all the women and children who were not being interviewed at the meeting house to remain in their homes until the situation with CPS and law enforcement was resolved.

Until then, I'd been taking photos independently, much to the displeasure of many men present. However, Uncle Isaac encouraged me to intensify documenting events. At 9:00 am, the police suddenly escalated their presence, bringing in the armored carrier, a stream of DPS (Texas Department of Public Safety) officers, Texas Rangers, Game Wardens, and multiple fully outfitted SWAT teams. They displayed large assault rifles openly. Despite this, I felt no fear, although I questioned their extensive display of weaponry in a peaceful community. Despite being a community of 600 inhabitants, the only weapons we had were a few hunting rifles locked in a single safe, which Uncle Isaac had immediately apprised them of upon their entry.

By 10:00 am, law enforcement decided to search all the homes, promising not to inspect the temple or our sacred sites in return. Upon hearing of the home searches, my older sister Lenora, called and urged me to visit her. I came to our house and asked what she needed. She requested I speak to Uncle Merril and retrieve a letter she had written him detailing private family issues. Initially questioning its importance, she assured me it contained nothing harmful but expressed her desire for it to remain private and not be confiscated by law enforcement.

Around 10 am, I sought Uncle Merril among state officials, including Texas Ranger Brooks Long, County Sheriff David Doran, Angie Voss, the head CPS Matron, and other officers. Waiting for an opportunity to ask about the letter, I overheard Uncle Merril telling Angie, who was overseeing the CPS investigation, that she held the power to turn the situation around. He implied, "You have the means, Angie. You can rectify this if you wish. Is Texas too proud now that you've proceeded this far, refusing to stop despite the repercussions?" Angie replied, "We've crossed a line, and there's no turning back." My heart sank when I heard this. I was dreadfully anxious for this to be over and return to normal life.

I had heard stories about the destruction of the Branch Davidian compound in Waco and hoped law enforcement wouldn't make similar mistakes. My older siblings had told me about law enforcement and FBI surrounding the Branch Davidian compound in Waco, Texas in 1993 in a raid they were conducting because of firearm violations. After a 51-day standoff, the compound had burned to the ground, killing nearly everyone inside. I had been told this happened because of egregious mistakes by law enforcement.

Eventually, Uncle Merril gave me directions to retrieve Lenora's letter from his wife, Aunt Barbara Jessop, who took care his office work. Lenora accompanied me and obtained her letter. Additionally, I removed my computer hard drive from my computer and stowed them in my coat pockets to prevent potential confiscation by law enforcement. I heard that law enforcement could take anything regardless of whether they needed it for their investigation or not.

As law enforcement conducted house searches, I entered the school where detained girls were held after questioning. I asked CPS workers if I could photograph them in the room they were being held in. Each directed me to Angie. Upon asking Angie, she denied my request abruptly. However, when the door was slightly open, the girls understood my intention. As soon as Angie left, Lisa Steed flung the door open, allowing me to quickly take a picture. Ruby Gutierrez, one of the CPS workers in the room, reacted angrily, scolding me for rudeness and slamming the door. Subsequently, several CPS workers and a police officer guarded the room, prompting me to continue photographing outside.

At this point, most of the girls eight years and older from our community had been brought to the Meeting House and been interviewed by CPS. Angie demanded Uncle Merril bring in four more girls or face escalated measures. She insisted on interviewing these girls, including the nonexistent Sarah Jessop Barlow and others whose names were found in the High School girls' English journals. Uncle Merril was unfamiliar the names they gave him. One was my sister Josephine Jeffs. He suggested he knew of a "Josie" Jeffs but not Josephine. Brooks Long warned of more extreme measures if the girls were not brought in. He said they would begin a more extensive search of the whole property until they found "Sarah." This led to growing frustration with law enforcement. We had no way to satisfy them that "Sarah" didn't exist. We felt like the "Sarah Jessop Barlow" allegation was a ploy they were using to conduct the raid.

Officers began searching houses thoroughly, examining every room, bathroom, closet, kitchen, and pantry, hunting for the elusive "Sarah." That day they were courteous enough to allow some of the workmen to accompany them on their searches.

Around noon, two Baptist Church buses arrived, piquing my curiosity about CPS's intentions. Despite questioning County Sheriff David Doran, he evaded explaining the buses' purpose. To alleviate our concerns, he invited a few boys, including myself, to inspect the armored personnel carrier. He explained it was available in case of victim rescue. I contested their quest for "Sarah Jessop Barlow," affirming no such person was present. Sheriff David Doran mentioned numerous calls alleging abuse at our location, but tracking the calls would take too much precious time. Unsatisfied, I stayed close, unconvinced by their explanations.

Angie Voss, accompanied by Sheriff Doran and other officers, entered the Meeting House and informed the mothers and girls interviewed that morning that the judge ordered them to relocate the girls to the Civic Center in Eldorado without their parents. No one had been prepared for CPS to come and interview the children. Many had never heard of them before. When they began the interviews, we realized there was something more they were trying to discover than this "Sarah Jessop Barlow." CPS refused to allow anyone to speak to the girls they had interviewed. Some girls gave information while others refused to speak or were devious in their answers, causing CPS a lot of confusion with the information they obtained. All of us mistrusted the motives of CPS and law enforcement.

The mothers vehemently resisted this decision. Sherriff Doran stepped out, conversed with Rich Jessop, and explained that CPS had decided it was in the best interest of the girls to remove them from the ranch. When they stepped back in the Meeting House, Rich dialed Uncle Merril and put him on speaker. Uncle Merril advised everyone to comply with the sheriff. Aunt Sally asked, "Should they go alone?" Uncle Merril replied, "Well, that's how they want it. I don't see another way." Doran assured them that CPS' number one priority was reuniting children with parents, affirmed by Angie's nod. Uncle Merril reiterated to cooperate. Tension mounted as no one moved. A little girl asked Doran if her mother could accompany her, but Doran explained she could not. He told her they were just taking a bus ride to Eldorado.

Mothers and girls clung to each other, sobbing intensely, especially the younger ones. The scene was filled with anxiety and fear. When tensions escalated, Doran asked if he should contact Uncle Merril again, and the mothers agreed. Doran called Uncle Merril back and put him on speakerphone. Uncle Merril emphasized cooperation with the sheriff and CPS. As he spoke, ReNae Jeffs, age 16, asked him, "Are we safe?" He simply replied, "Well, we hope and pray you are." Doran informed Uncle Merril of their plans, and the separation began, marking the commencement of Texas CPS' infamous saga.

Amid escalating emotions, the crying and noise intensified. CPS gathered more girls from another room, who were unaware of the situation, to join the others in boarding the buses. Mothers accompanied their girls onto the bus, many younger ones crying and pleading not to go without their mothers. Despite their pleas, CPS refused their entreaties. Once on the bus, the mothers pled again with CPS to let them accompany their daughters. CPS stubbornly refused.

I witnessed the heart-wrenching scene of parents being separated from their children. The profound anguish and fear I experienced and observed during the forced separation left me deeply angered at the state's actions. It seemed unjust. I questioned whether there could have been a better way to address the situation if something truly grave was at hand. Law enforcement continued to demand we turn over "Sarah" whom they alleged was being sexually abused and beaten. We continued to affirm to them that she was nonexistent, but they refused to believe us. It appeared CPS and law enforcement thought they were saving the girls. The scene, capable of moving the most callous hearts, failed to stir the state officials.

At 2 pm, following the girls' departure, Jim Jessop and I approached Ranger Brooks Long, expressing our dismay. He cited "doing his job" and following orders, emphasizing obedience to their superiors. As more men gathered around him, questioning the state's response, he grew uneasy, so we left him.

Meanwhile, David Doran returned from escorting the buses to Eldorado. He shared his reluctance in having to participate in the girl's separation and told us of his efforts to prevent a temple search. He reassured us they would respect our sacred sites. Mother Annette sought assurance that she would not be separated from her children but was informed it was beyond his control. Doran provided Lynn McFadden's contact information, the CPS worker involved in the affidavit and the search warrant, if we desired more details about CPS's decisions.

Upon concluding our conversation with the sheriff, I went to our house and showed Grandmother Merilyn, Father's mother, the pictures and videos I had taken of the separation and removal of the girls. While in her office, Father called our land-line telephone from jail in Kingman, AZ. I spoke to him and informed him of the girls' removal. Grandmother Merilyn told him we were undergoing a raid with hundreds of law enforcement on the land. He then asked to be put on speaker. He reminded his family that in the 1953 raid on Short Creek, AZ, the women and children of the community refused to testify against their fathers and husbands. He referenced us to a sermon of Leroy Johnson, a former leader of the group and told us to read it that night.

After Father hung up, a group of us boys sat on the lawn by Father's house, reminiscing with each other about the different facets of the ongoing raid. As we were doing this, Ranger Nick Hanna approached, requesting access to the storehouse, the central place of the community where everyone received all their food, clothing, and home goods. We told Nick Hanna we would not consent to his entry, but if he was determined to get in, he could pick the lock with a knife instead of breaking it.

By 3 pm, we were very frustrated with the whole raid and started telling the officers that we did not give our consent for them to search anywhere in the community or on the ranch, as we felt like our First and Fourth Amendment rights were being violated. We believed Judge Walther was overstepping her bounds in issuing a blanket search warrant for an entire community and believed it was based off bias against our religion. The officers responded that they had a search warrant for the entire ranch and were determined to carry it out.

Chapter Five

"We Demand a Lawyer!"

At 4 pm, April 4, 2008, law enforcement regrouped at the school and received instructions. They had searched all the houses except Father's and Uncle Merril's. Both homes were large. Father's was approximately 25,000 square feet. Uncle Merril's was closer to 18,000. After receiving directions, a large group of officers walked toward our house. We followed them, and when they reached our patio, SWAT team leader Sean Palmer split the officers into squads and sent them in several directions. He requested us boys not to interfere and stay away so we wouldn't be harmed.

Law enforcement officers scattered in all directions. Groups of officers surrounded our house. Many were stationed along the North and South sides. Some were positioned on the road, blocking it off. Another large group headed towards Uncle Merril's house. We observed that nearly every officer carried multiple gun magazines and was prepared for combat, holding their assault rifles.

It was now 4:10 pm. I followed two squads of officers until they reached the front of our house. A SWAT team positioned themselves on the deck at the parlor door. Two officers stood against the log wall on the south side of the door, while another stood on the North side, with their rifles ready. A fourth officer stood at the center of the door and began banging on it. A similar team was positioned below the deck at the Sewing Room door. While they banged, they shouted, "POLICE, open it up!! POLICE! OPEN THE DOOR!"

Louis Jessop had gone up on the deck with the officers, so they asked him for a key. He replied that he did not have one. The officers then ordered him off the deck, saying it was too dangerous.

No one would answer the doors. Everyone in our family had gathered in the living room and begun singing to help calm the children's fears. As the officers grew increasingly exasperated, Mother Millie opened the parlor door. The officers beside the door aimed their guns at her. She demanded, "Put your guns down!" Her four-year-old son Merril looked up at her and asked, "Are they coming to kill us?" At that moment, I ran around to the back to slip into the house before all the doors were blocked. On my way, I met my high school friend William Nielsen, my brother Levi, and Louis Jessop. I handed Mitchel's camera to William and instructed them to follow me. We entered through the Southwest door near my grandmother's office. Despite the intensity of the situation, I wanted to be in the house to make sure my family would be safe and protected.

I arrived at the living room where our family had gathered, just as Texas Ranger John Nick Hanna and his team entered. He seemed to be one of the officers in charge. Law enforcement quickly swarmed into the house and initiated a search. They prohibited anyone from leaving the living room. Our house had more than 30 bedrooms, so it was more like searching a hotel.

Jim Jessop advised the family to remain silent, only refusing consent for the search and demanding a lawyer, as instructed by some attorneys Uncle Merril had hired earlier that day to represent us.

Mother Annette, Father's first wife, and Mother Paula, who had previously been married to my grandfather, were present, prepared to address law enforcement. When Texas Ranger Nick Hanna approached the living room door, Mother Annette informed him, "We do not consent to the search of this house!" He acknowledged her stance, explained their purpose, and mentioned this was one of the final houses they were searching. He emphasized that despite their lack of consent, the search would proceed due to the judge's order. Despite his explanation, she reiterated, "But I still don't consent!"

Following this, they requested everyone to gather in one place, and those in the hall moved into the living room. There was nearly 100 of us in there. Our living room was the size of a small meeting hall. Meanwhile, officers intensified their search efforts. CPS had arrived at the house and was directed into the living room.

An older CPS worker named Susan stepped forward with a microphone to inform us of their intentions. She announced they would be taking all children under the age of eighteen, "except for maybe the teenage boys," away from the ranch for interviews. We expressed considerable dissatisfaction with them coming in with so much law enforcement. She said they were removing the children and interviewing them so they could find out what the situation was on the ranch. CPS made this decision, because they were having a hard time determining the ages of the mothers and which mothers each child belonged to. We asked her what CPS' concern was. She replied, "There's a lot of concerns, but that's what we need to talk to the children about." We knew they had not given themselves the time nor had the staff necessary for ascertaining who all the children and mothers in the community were before making this decision. There were 416 children on the ranch and nearly 140 mothers. They had made the decision to upend a small town with 25 separate dwellings, many of them housing several families, in less than 24 hours. We felt this was extremely irrational.

At this point, CPS had been to nearly all the other homes in the community and had not removed any children besides the girls who were at the meeting house. We had hoped they would allow us to stay.

While CPS addressed us, Law Enforcement attempted to search Father's separate apartment area. It consisted of his room, office, and waiting room. After the house was complete, he had a few select workers double-insulate his area and expand his sub-apartment. They built a tiny set of stairs to two more large rooms downstairs. The downstairs rooms were remodeled to include a small kitchen, bedroom, and ordinance room. Only Father's most trusted wives were allowed into this area. He claimed Jesus himself came to his room and gave him revelations. Most of us weren't allowed to see into this apartment. Father was an extremely secretive man. A few of the mothers contested the search, considering his area sacred. After some negotiation, the police relented and did not search his area that day. But now their suspicions had been aroused. We felt an extremely thorough search of the ranch was looming.

After Susan finished speaking, CPS informed us that mothers could accompany the children this time. Many family members began to comply, and Tina Martinez, another CPS worker, asked to handle one household at a time. We clarified we were all one family.

Jim Jessop, visibly frustrated, and wanting to protect the "prophet's" family, declared, "We demand a lawyer!" which led everyone to echo, "WE DEMAND A LAWYER!" He then instructed everyone to sit back down.

CPS seemed taken aback. Tina Martinez offered us the option of seeking a lawyer from the phone book. They then threatened to forcibly take the children, reiterating that mothers could join if they wished. Once more, we collectively demanded a lawyer. CPS stated they had an order from

Judge Walther to remove the children. Jim insisted they present and read us the order. After conferring among themselves, CPS claimed they had already shown it to Uncle Merril.

Knowing we had already hired a lawyer named Nathan Butler, I asked Jim Jessop to call Mr. Butler on his cell phone. He did so, and Mr. Butler advised us to follow the judge's order and allow CPS to take the children without interfering.

While he was on the phone, Tina Martinez mentioned, "Just so you know, we're allowing the mothers to come, which is more than we usually do. It's something exceptional. We want to gather the children, let us talk to them, and return them to you. That's what we're aiming for." This set the mother's more at ease as they felt this was a promise that their children wouldn't be taken from them.

Tina Martinez then asked if she could speak to Mr. Butler. The service cut out just after Jim handed his phone to her, so I handed my cell phone to them, and they both used it to talk to Mr. Butler. After their conversation, we all realized the children would have to go. Ashley Sayles, another CPS worker, stepped up and announced, "If the mothers want to come with their children, then you're welcome to." After watching the first group of girls being taken away, we were relieved that CPS was now allowing the mothers to accompany their children.

Everyone stood up, and the children gathered in groups with their mothers. Some mothers had gone to Kingman, Arizona to visit Father in jail, so their children joined with other mothers. At this point, I felt inclined to ask if I could go with my siblings despite being one of the teenage boys. I informed Ashley Sayles that I was 17 and asked if I could accompany my mother's children. She consented. I handed over the camcorder to my brother Levi, informing him that I was leaving and asking him to manage it. Then, I gathered with my mother's and Mother Annette's children. We inquired whether we needed to bring a change of clothes. They said it wasn't necessary, and we'd likely be back late that night. Nonetheless, several mothers brought their children's clothes; all I brought with me were the clothes on my back. We brought a few blankets, our cell phones, charging cords, notebooks, a few religious texts, and hymn books.

Many of the children and mothers needed their shoes before leaving. When Father had first established the community, he made a rule that no one wear their outside shoes inside any of the homes, so the houses would remain clean. We placed our shoes on specially constructed shelves by each outside door. The officers forbade anyone from going anywhere to retrieve shoes or anything else. When Abraham attempted to run downstairs for his shoes, an officer yelled at him, "Kiddo, get back up here! If you go down there, you'll get shot!" Abe quickly scurried back upstairs. Eventually, a CPS worker took him downstairs to help him find his shoes. The officers finally allowed Jim Jessop to collect the shoes. He gathered them from outside and brought as many as he could in a box for everyone to search through and find their pair.

CPS workers slowly escorted us in small groups out to the buses. Many officers were milling around, and most of the men were gathered near the buses, observing. We sat in the buses for about an hour while CPS gathered the children and mothers from Uncle Merril's, Leroy Steed's, and Marion Steed's homes.

At 5:45 pm, we departed from our community in a line of buses with a police escort. As the bus I was in left the property, we started singing hymns to bring comfort to one another and pacify the traumatized children. We passed many officers along the county road. At the highway intersection, the media were present. CPS workers instructed us not to look at them and cover our faces with a pillow if available "for our safety." Instead, everyone attempted to see the reporters as we drove by. We traveled through Eldorado and arrived at the Civic Center located on the south side of the small town.

Chapter Six

Eldorado Civic Center

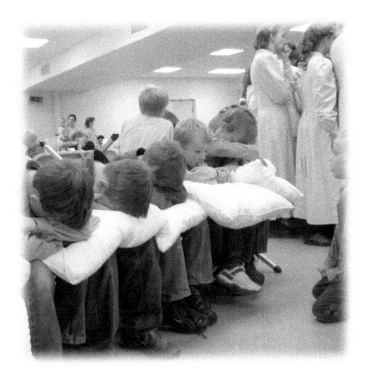

The Civic Center in Eldorado is a large metal building that is about 10,700 square feet. It contains several large rooms, a kitchen, and several public restrooms.

When the buses pulled into the parking lot of the Civic Center, the sheriff asked us to wait inside the bus for a few minutes while they made final preparations for our arrival. Then, Sheriff Doran led us into the Civic Center. We were placed in a large rectangular room on the North end of the building. The room contained only three long rows of tables with chairs. All the windows were covered with plastic to prevent anyone from seeing in or out. George, the sheriff's deputy, approached me, provided his phone number and quietly said, "If you need any help, just call me."

Shortly after our arrival, instead of being immediately taken in for interviews, we were provided dinner by the Salvation Army. It consisted of soup, chicken nuggets, corn dogs, potato chips, and fruit punch. We were not accustomed to processed food, but feeling hungry, we ate heartily. Some of the mothers and children feared there was poison in the fruit punch. Once they saw CPS drink it, their fears departed. Around this time, Leroy Jessop's family arrived at the Civic Center and joined us.

Through a window in the door, we could see across the entry into another large room where they detained the group of girls who had been removed earlier that day. Many in our group began waving to them, prompting CPS to cover those windows with plastic as well. CPS informed us that our group must remain separate from them until all were interviewed. Soon after, they informed us that they were taking the girls and Leroy Steed's family over to the Baptist Church.

There was much noise and confusion among the children as there was nothing for them to do. The young boys gathered around me, inquiring of me about the raid. They had stayed at home until CPS removed us from the ranch. A CPS worker named Mary approached us, and we asked her when we would get return home. She said it would probably be in the morning. Since there were no beds or bedding in the room, I assumed we would all be sleeping on the concrete floor that night. Some of the mothers began arranging the youngest children on the tables. At this time, CPS began conducting interviews, which lasted until 10 pm.

Around 8:00 pm, staff started bringing in many cots. An older man and two ladies began setting them up. We boys asked if we could help and joined in assembling many cots. Thin blankets, sleeping bags, and small vinyl pillows were brought in. Everyone found a cot and began settling down in the large room. Very few had brought a change of clothes. Many of us had cell phones so we found outlets for charging them. There were no toiletries there besides the accommodations of the public restrooms in the building. My brothers and I put all our cots together in one area. I was the oldest male there.

At 9:00 pm, a few of the mothers asked me to lead a prayer and read the sermon of Leroy Johnson that Father had recommended. Mother Esther provided me with a book. Standing by a lectern, I led the prayer and began reading. The sermon was one and a half pages long.

When I was about halfway through, I noticed two State Troopers entering. They walked up to me and said, "Come with us, young man." I closed the book, set it down, and followed them. They led me out of the room to where many CPS officials were gathered. They inquired who I was and why I was there. I informed them that I had received permission from CPS and expressed my willingness to cooperate. Initially, they were about to send me back home and told me to find someone who could come get me, but at the last minute, they turned me over to CPS.

A tall lady took me into the mechanical room for my interview. She asked for my name and my mother's name. I provided this information and mentioned that my mother had passed away, and my mother's children were under the guardianship of Mother Annette. However, I declined to give my father's name, following the instructions our mothers gave us to protect our fathers and not disclose any information about them. The interview proceeded with these questions:

"Are you married?"

"Of course not!"

"What do you mean, 'of course not'? In Texas, it's legal to be married at age 17."

"Well, I'm not."

"Do you people court and date girls?"

"I don't know what everyone else does, but I sure don't."(Dating and courting was forbidden in FLDS culture. All marriages were strictly arranged by Father.)

"What is the age you can get married?"

"Eighteen or so."

"So, you turn eighteen, and something just happens?"

"Yeah."

At that point, I became uneasy and didn't want the interview to include questions that I felt I could not answer without betraying Father. Father taught that providing any information about him to gentiles or apostates was turning traitor and was the worst sin we could commit. Doing so would consign us to the lowest hell. I decided to end the interview, so I yawned and mentioned, "I stayed up all night last night and haven't slept yet."

"Oh, you must be pretty tired."

"Yes."

"I haven't had the chance to be there. How's it been going there?"

I gave her a brief account of the searches and our removal. Subsequently, she said she would check with CPS regarding what they wanted me to do and had me follow her. As we were walking, I mentioned to her that the mothers and children in the other room really wanted me to stay. She positioned me close to where CPS officials were gathered and gave me a chair by the wall to sit on. I remained there while they discussed my fate among themselves.

In a few minutes, a CPS man came over and informed me that I would be staying. He fetched a cot and led me back into the mechanical room, designating it as my sleeping space for the night. He provided me with a thin blanket, a vinyl pillow, and a chair for himself. The room's lights were turned off, and he settled himself at the foot of my cot. I had my cell phone in my pocket, but realized I needed to be discreet with its use from now on. The door to the room on the south was left open with the lights on, while the door on the north, leading to the room where everyone else were sleeping was closed and chained shut. As I lay there, I listened to those in the large room singing for quite some time, and a sense of peace enveloped us. Eventually, the children became calm, and all was quiet. I lay there, wondering how they thought I could be such a threat. I assumed it was because I had conducted the prayer and reading. "Maybe they think I'm some leader that slipped in and was trying to control everyone. How come these people think so much different than us?" I thought.

Frightened, I remained completely still all night, though I slept very little. The room became quite cold, and my blanket offered little warmth. Throughout the night, my guard left a few times, but never for long. During those moments, I took the opportunity to adjust my position and try to keep warm. The room had no windows, so I couldn't discern when morning arrived, nor did I dare look at my watch. It felt like the longest night. When I heard movement in the larger room and the children began to make noise, I sat up on my cot. The guard smiled and informed me I could return to the other room, which surprised me. All night, I had been afraid CPS would keep me isolated from my family until the raid was over. Glancing at my watch, I saw it was exactly 6:00 am.

Day 3

Upon returning to the large room where everyone gathered, CPS announced breakfast was ready. We lined up and were served food by the Salvation Army. I attempted to eat the pasty oatmeal dish they provided but couldn't manage it. Shortly after, they brought us some dry cereal, which was more palatable. Following breakfast, they resumed the interviews. However, most of the children and mothers declined to answer their questions.

When we caught wind that CPS was starting to remove children from the community, word had gone around to all the families to make a concerted effort to stop answering their questions and giving them any information. We were afraid they were trying to destroy our religion and remove and scatter the children, just as Arizona had attempted on our grandparents in 1953.

In July of 1953, the state of Arizona had conducted a week-long raid on the community of Short Creek. Nearly all the married men and several of the grandmothers of the community were taken to jail in Kingman, AZ. Then the state had removed approximately 60 mothers and 263 children from the community, scattering them across the state. It took two years of court battles before the people of the community prevailed and were able to return home. Many of these people were now our grandparents. Some of the grandmothers at the ranch were the mothers in the 1953 raid. They had already lived through this before. The '53 raid was partially responsible for the secretive, insular life we now lived under. It was hard to trust that any governmental agency had our best interests at heart.

As the morning progressed, we noticed certain CPS workers trying to engage us in friendly conversations, feigning interest. We soon realized they were attempting to extract more information from us, prompting us to be much more cautious in what we said and did. We were closely and continuously monitored. Whenever we inquired about returning home, CPS assured us we would be going back soon.

After the interviews concluded, CPS allowed the children to enter another large room to play games like throwing balls, jumping rope, and engaging in activities until lunchtime and after lunch until approximately 2:00 pm. They also permitted us to go outside briefly, but after ten minutes, the media discovered us, and we were promptly ushered back inside.

With the interviews complete, we were perplexed, wondering why we couldn't return home now, as several CPS workers had led us to believe we would. CPS now informed us we could not return until the search by law enforcement on the ranch was complete. Apparently, more warrants had been obtained and law enforcement was seeking to search the temple. Our attorneys tried contesting it, but Judge Walther ruled that it had to happen, even if we considered it a sacred place.

During this period, we received several phone calls from home informing us that law enforcement was attempting to breach the temple, because we refused to open any gates or doors for them. We were told they would be attempting to scale the temple walls at 3:00 pm, so we all gathered in the room and prayed. At home, our men were stationed around the sacred sites, instructed to kneel in prayer when law enforcement initiated the attempt to breach the temple walls. At the Civic Center, we formed a large circle and prayed. Subsequently, we all remained on our knees, occasionally engaging in vocal prayer, followed by moments of silent prayer. Everyone, even the youngest children, were weeping and fervently praying for God to protect the temple from being desecrated. Father had told us that if we were united and sinless, God would strike down anyone that attempted to enter the temple unlawfully.

Father also taught that if anyone not appointed by him were to enter the temple, God would reject us and our temple. We knelt for at least an hour, deeply concerned that some of the men at home might lose their lives by resisting the warrant and standing in the way.

A few of the mothers asked one of the CPS staff if we could have more privacy while we prayed for the temple's protection. They acquiesced and the mothers stood up many cots on end in a circle, hiding us from their sight. When the CPS staff in charge saw this, they angrily ordered us to take the cots down. They brought several state troopers in to monitor us, uneasy about what our reaction would be if the temple was breached.

Around 5:30 pm, family members from home called us on our cell phones and informed us that law enforcement were now preparing to breach the temple walls, break into the temple and search it. We gathered again in prayer, hoping for a miracle. We were terrified that we would be rejected by God.

After the prayer, I called a friend at home who was by the temple walls, and he let me listen to the officers banging on the temple doors with a sledgehammer until they broke it open. This took them about 40 minutes. When I realized it was over, I was filled with anguish that this had happened. I had helped with the construction of that building and considered it the House of the Lord. I didn't believe anything evil would ever happen in there.

Just after this, CPS came in and demanded we allow them to physically examine everyone under 18 years of age. We were distraught by this time and vehemently opposed this, so they did not carry it out. (In our culture, we were taught from our youngest years that having our bodies uncovered in front of others was defiling our body unless it was an absolute medical emergency) They had just violated our beautiful, majestic temple. Now they wanted to violate the temple of our body.

Late that evening, CPS asked if they could take us in small groups to the high school to shower, but we also refused this as we believed it to be a ruse to break us up and separate us. There began to be a widening gap of mistrust between CPS and us. Nothing had made it so bad as the desecration of the temple. Everyone was extremely irritable at this point.

After the many experiences of this day, the children were finally settled by 10:00 pm, with the older girls singing hymns to calm the younger children. Our attorneys came to the Civic Center but were not allowed inside. The mothers went out in several groups, one at a time, to speak with them. This continued until 1:00 am. During this time, I managed to call my sisters Rachel and Melanie, who were in the community Father had established in South Dakota and informed them about all that was happening.

As we were finally getting ready for bed, Mother Ruthie had a seizure; a chronic condition she was dealing with. The mothers surrounded her to shield her from CPS observation. CPS turned on the lights. Only after several pleas did they turn off the lights and allow the mothers to handle the situation. "Could anything else go wrong today?" I thought. Just a few minutes later, one of the mothers let out a terrified scream that startled us all, which turned into laughter when we realized it was because a toad was in her cup of water.

By the end of this day, all the children were very sad and kept asking when we would go back home. CPS kept informing us that it would be on Monday when the search would be over. Throughout the day, several more mothers and children were added to our group, totaling 140 people, all sleeping in this room on the cots provided for us. I compiled a list of everyone in our group, which I kept in my pocket (until we were scattered throughout the state. I still have the list.) The constant concern on our minds was the potential separation of children from their mothers, as we overheard several comments from CPS workers hinting at this goal.

Day 4

The next morning, we attempted to hold Sunday school at 9:00 am. Despite the noise, different families sang songs, and we had scripture readings afterward. However, CPS interrupted and instructed us to immediately gather our belongings and prepare to be bused to a better facility in San Angelo. We closed Sunday school, gathered our few belongings, and the children grouped with their mothers.

We safely boarded the bus and were soon on our way. During the journey, we sang several songs. Upon our arrival in San Angelo, fifty miles from the ranch, I called my cousin, Luke Jeffs, informing him of each street we turned on so family members staying close by would know our whereabouts. We finally arrived at a place called Fort Concho by 12:00 pm, about twenty minutes after those who had come from the Baptist church in Eldorado. These were the girls who were first taken into state custody.

Chapter Seven

Fort Concho

F ort Concho is a former United States Army installation that was established in 1867 at the confluence of the North and South Concho Rivers. It was an active military base for 22 years and the troops stationed there had participated in several Indian wars. It is now a National Historic Landmark District and has been owned and operated by the city of San Angelo since 1935.

Back at the ranch, family members called and informed us that CPS was now removing everyone under 18 years of age and taking them into custody. They were allowing the mothers to come with their children. Everyone was going to be brought to Fort Concho. Most of the girls who had been taken first were still separated from their parents and other siblings and were full of hope that they would now be reunited. CPS would not allow this.

CPS took all of us into a large stone building they called "Shelter 2", where they had just brought all the girls from the Baptist Church, making a total of 221 people in that building. Shelter 2 had one large room they put us in. This room also had a large loft. Initially, they refused to allow anyone on the upstairs loft. There were hundreds of cots prepared and spread across the floor in rows, with narrow walkways between them. CPS officials were stationed all through the building, monitoring our activities and attempting to overhear our conversations. The room felt congested, like a traffic jam. The noise was tremendous, with children crying, shouting, and running around. No one was permitted outside, and the children hardly knew how to channel their pent-up energy. Our frustration with CPS's stringent rules only intensified.

After an hour, CPS permitted some of the boys to go up to the loft for a few minutes. Unfortunately, one of the boys threw some items off the loft, which prompted Uncle Merril to call me and inquire about reports of the boys behaving wildly and tossing things around. He hinted that CPS had sent this report of the boys misbehaving through his attorneys. Consequently, none of the boys were allowed up there after that incident. Later, CPS allowed several mothers and children to use the loft area for their living quarters. My brothers and I chose to settle under the loft, with my cot placed in the northwest corner against the outside wall.

Shortly afterward, CPS granted us access to the adjacent building labeled Shelter 1. As soon as they assured us that both groups could interact, about a third of our group relocated to that building, providing us with more breathing room.

Around this time, a CPS lady was tailing Mother Kate because she had a bag containing journals kept by several members of our group since being in state custody. I noticed this and intentionally blocked the CPS lady a couple of times, which she didn't appreciate. She then conferred with other CPS officials about it, and a couple of them began tailing me.

CPS announced the availability of a trailer equipped with showers for us to use. A bag of clothes had been sent to me from home through law enforcement, and I was eager for a shower since I had gone several sweaty days without one. Mother Annette informed me that the boys were next in line, so I gathered my clothes and was heading out there when I heard two CPS officials mention my departure and pick up their phones. Instead of going out to the showers, I went into the bathroom inside the building and used dampened paper towels for a sponge bath instead of going out to have a shower. I couldn't decide if they were trying to remove me from the fort or take me somewhere else. I retired to my cot for a few hours so I could get out from under the CPS spotlight.

On the same day, the remaining families from home arrived in other shelters at Ft. Concho but were prohibited from having any contact with us. We could see many of them housed in a building about 150 feet away from shelter one. Initially restricted from going outside, later in the afternoon, CPS allowed eight of us at a time to venture out and run around. Eventually, everyone else joined us outside, and the rule was lifted. Dinner was served at 8:00 pm under large canopies that had been set up.

After dinner, several state troopers showed up and demanded all the cell phones. One of them walked up to Mother Annette, who was outside, and confiscated hers while she was talking to her attorney. My sister Josephine quickly came and informed me about what was happening. I hurried over to my cot, placed my phone in my clothing bag, and approached one of the officers who were collecting phones to see what they were up to. He immediately demanded to know if I had a phone and asked what was in my pockets. I turned my pockets inside out so he could see. All I had was my comb and Mother Annette's keys that she had asked me to keep. There was a small pocketknife on the key ring, which the officer asked me to give up. Shortly after, another officer approached me and demanded my phone, and I went through the same procedure with him. Mother Kate gave them a tough time about taking her phone so others in the building could have time to hide theirs. However, most of the cell phones were confiscated that evening, and from then on, I had to be extremely cautious about using mine. I charged it secretly at night. My phone was able to hold a charge for about three days.

I went to bed at midnight. From the time we arrived, we conducted our own night watch to carefully oversee the safety of all the children. We were terrified that CPS would try separating us during the night.

Often at night, several CPS officials would walk around through the cots, counting everyone, but the older girls would quietly move around, and they always failed to get an accurate count.

Day 5

The next morning, we rose and engaged in prayer and reading. Throughout the day, CPS persistently tried to extract more information from us, attempting to listen in on our conversations, but we refused to divulge anything. We learned how to communicate without moving our lips because we noticed them trying to lip-read. We didn't cooperate with them much due to them lying to us about being returned home and bringing parents and siblings back together. Various BCFS (Baptist Child and Family Services) staff and volunteers from around the country were present. We swiftly discerned the distinction between CPS and the other groups there, and we had a lot more trust in these volunteer groups.

San Angelo police and State Troopers surrounded the entire area and were often a source of fun and entertainment to the unstoppable curiosity of the children. The children spent almost the entire day playing in a small sandy area behind Shelter 2. By the day's end, frustration was palpable for everyone. We were very upset about still being held in custody and wondered when law enforcement would be leaving the ranch. We thought CPS was going to allow us to return after they were through there. They hadn't told us they were working hard to prevent our return.

Through the day, it became evident to us that they genuinely intended to separate the mothers and children based on many conversations we overheard between CPS workers discussing this. Additionally, my 15-year-old sister Josephine and I observed approximately 16 Greyhound buses arriving and parking nearby. After dinner that night, a CPS worker named Ashley Sayles stated that they wanted to gather the names and ages of all the children. We staunchly refused, fearing that their motive for obtaining this information was to separate us.

Day 6

On the morning of April 8, our relationship with CPS continued deteriorating. All of us united in not giving CPS any information, and any trust that had been there at the beginning was gone. We still had no information from them on why they were holding us for so long, except they still hadn't found the nonexistent "Sarah Jessop Barlow," and law enforcement wasn't finished with the search.

Since my experience of isolation the first night in the Civic Center, I had been very careful not to wander much, and others would bring me the meals served outside under two large canopies. However, this morning, I decided to go out and get my own breakfast. Before I had been there long, a San Angelo police officer questioned my presence, suspecting I had sneaked in. I informed her I was 17 and that CPS was aware of my presence. She was unsatisfied and had me stay close to another officer while she sought clarification from CPS. After five or ten minutes, she returned and confirmed my clearance. This made so I could be freer in going outside in the boundaries they had given us.

Several more buses arrived, so Josephine and I approached nearly every CPS official and inquired about the buses' purpose. They all claimed ignorance. When we walked away, we overheard one of them asking another, "What are we supposed to say when they ask us questions like that?" We feared what their purpose was and frustrated to no end about the whole removal from the ranch. We were terrified that CPS was hatching a plan to separate us from our parents and each other.

Mid-morning, Texas Rangers Wende Wakeman and Laura Simmons came and held a parley with Mother Annette, Mother Paula, and Aunt Barbara Jessop, explaining to them the importance of some cooperation with CPS and the need to provide information on all the mothers and children. At 11:00 am, they and CPS reached an agreement with these three mothers to provide the names of all the mothers and their children along with their dates of birth. That afternoon, the trio went with the Rangers to all the other shelters to persuade the mothers there to cooperate.

Around noon, I took my phone into the bathroom and turned it on. Many text messages came in from family members, frantic to know if we had been separated from our mothers. One message was sent from family in Kingman, AZ, which they had received from Father. It stated, "If they try taking the children from the mothers, don't resist or fight them. They won't be gone long."

Late that evening, the Rangers returned with the mothers and addressed us, promising to attempt to retrieve the phones that had been confiscated from us. They told us law enforcement was about to leave the ranch. We asked why they were there so long, and they told us they were gathering evidence of any criminal activity, especially pertaining to any abuse of children. We laughed and told them we were sure there wasn't any. The parents weren't laughing, however, because of the strain they were under. They were also concerned legal action would be taken against some of their husbands, because there were several of these men who had been given underage wives by Father with whom they'd had children.

Father had taught us that the government purposefully made laws against underage marriage so they could persecute us. He claimed to be following God's dictates whenever he arranged a marriage and stated only God could decide what the right age for marriage was. He asserted he would be disobeying God were he to obey the laws of man and perform no underage marriages. When Father married young girls, he declared God had shown him wicked men were trying to ravish and kill those girls. He claimed to be their savior.

Because I was a boy, I knew I wouldn't be married until I was at least eighteen. No male in the church was allowed to be married until he was ordained an Elder, an office in the Priesthood. That usually happened at eighteen years or older, so I hadn't thought much about the underage factor, although it always bothered me to see the girls who were my own classmates get married off when they were so young.

When we asked if CPS was going to let us go home soon, the Rangers avoided giving any clear answer. Simultaneously, all the Greyhound buses departed. Months later, we discovered that the state's plan to bus us about 300 miles away to Midlothian, Texas, to a large Salvation Army facility and separate the mothers and children was foiled as the Salvation Army organization refused this action on their premises, leading to the plan's failure.

Day 7

The following day, around 8:00 am, CPS announced they would conduct physical exams. They reasoned that they needed to do this to see if there had been any physical abuse, although there was no reason to suspect this. We felt like this was turning into a witch hunt. Everyone vehemently refused. I observed that the strain was beginning to show on many of the mothers. Most looked like they had only minimal sleep since we had been removed from home.

Not much occurred until after lunch when a BCFS worker gathered us at 3:00 pm and informed us about a tornado watch from 5:00 pm until 10:00 pm. She instructed us that in case of a tornado warning and if time permitted, they would take us to the City Hall; otherwise, we were to assemble by the center wall in our shelter and take cover under our cots.

Soon after, the rangers collected the names, ages, and dates of birth of the mothers and their children. They claimed this was an effort to reunite mothers with their children, especially those with children in different shelters. They had everyone go outside until they completed collecting the information. At the same time, the mothers were served legal papers explaining why their children were removed and were given their first court dates. These court documents filed by CPS stated that CPS had made reasonable efforts, consistent with time and circumstances prior to our removal to prevent or eliminate the need for removal of the children. It also claimed CPS had made reasonable efforts to make it possible for the children to return to their homes. These claims were ridiculous. CPS literally walked into our home and removed us without interviewing a single child in our house or determining any of the circumstances there.

The papers also claimed there was a continuing danger to the physical health and safety of the children if they were to be returned to their parents. They stated that the children had been victims of sexual abuse and there was evidence that if they were to be returned home, there were adults residing in the homes that had seriously abused or neglected the children. CPS asserted the abuse was likely to continue. CPS was branding a whole community for the underage marriages that had happened and justifying the removal of all the children because of this regardless of whether they were in danger or not.

As a side note, CPS could have easily confirmed there would be no more underage marriages without Father being there to perform the ceremony, and he was already locked up in prison. Why they didn't focus on the evidence of criminal activity that he had caused on the ranch instead of removing all the children is baffling.

It was obvious the children were much happier and healthier at home. Father had previously broken up some families among the FLDS, but years later, Father would escalate this to the level of what CPS did at the ranch and in the shelters. The way the raid was being conducted would only give Father more power and control over the FLDS people. The state was confirming our conviction that we were being persecuted because we were God's people and were doing God's will. Father had repeatedly prophesied of greater persecution coming upon us and it was happening. Now we were more determined than ever to obey his mandates. The raid became proof of his position as "God's Holy

Prophet."

After this process, the rangers returned phones to the adults. We began to think maybe the Texas Rangers were there to help us go back home soon and started trusting them more.

Our food was poor and consisted mostly of chicken and potatoes for lunch and dinner each day. There were many volunteers from around the state assisting, but CPS hadn't expected there to be so many women and children on the ranch and the state hadn't been prepared for this large of a group to be removed.

During the day, we would move cots aside in the center of the building so the children could color pictures and play. CPS allowed a table with snacks to be provided inside the shelter during the daytime.

Mother Annette informed me that Father had sent a message expressing gratitude for my presence at the shelters and instructing me to conduct prayers and readings with the people in our shelter. He was able to pass information secretly through one of his attorneys to his brother Nephi, who then gave it to Mother Naomie. Mother Naomie called Mother Annette with this information. We considered it important to have someone who bore the priesthood be with any group of our people. All males in the church were given the Aaronic Priesthood around age 12, like the LDS church. If they were faithful to the church, they could advance and be ordained an Elder in the Melchizedek Priesthood at age 18. These weren't leadership positions. The leaders were given higher offices in the Priesthood. I was the only boy in this group who was of age and had been given the Aaronic Priesthood. A man or boy with the priesthood taking charge of pastoral duties was considered the proper way in our culture, even if he was not an adult. If there was a gathering for prayer or a meeting, a priesthood bearer was always asked to take charge if he was present.

That night, after settling all the children into bed, I positioned myself near the window under the loft, close to my cot, observing the weather. It was evident that a storm was approaching, and I loved storm-watching. Nearby, there was a door leading to a room where several CPS officials and other staff members were conversing loudly, evidently listening to a weather radio. Just after 11:00 pm, I heard an alarm sound from their radio, followed by their frantic reactions as they hurried to the main room where we were situated. Shortly afterward, the tornado sirens across the city began blaring, audible to all of us.

The shelter transformed into a scene of chaos, with lights flickering on and off, mothers waking their sleeping children, confused cries from kids, and personnel instructing everyone to gather by the center wall. Despite the confusion, everyone eventually found a place by the wall, sitting on the cots. The staff, clearly anxious, urged us to cover our heads with pillows or take shelter under the cots. A guard shouted for me and the younger boys to move away from the window as it was unsafe. But my fascination with the storm kept me glued to the window, engrossed in the powerful winds and vivid lightning flashes amidst the pouring rain. It was unmistakably a tornado-like storm with strong rotation. Teresa and Josephine remarked, "If we were home, we'd be on the deck watching!" An elderly gentleman reassured us, noting the strength of the building against many storms.

Eventually, the noise subsided, and the gentleman suggested singing.

Everyone joined in singing hymns: "Master the Tempest is Raging" and "Dearest Children, God is Near You." After forty minutes, the storm passed, and calmness returned. I stepped outside, where the wind was still fierce, and talked to an officer who had stayed out during the storm. Branches littered the ground, and one of the canopies had blown away. I captured a few pictures with my phone before returning indoors. Some of the girls ventured outside to take pictures, but the night staff ordered everyone back in. Before retiring for the night, we gathered for prayer, expressing gratitude for the Lord's protection.

Day 8

On April 10, CPS came again for the medical exams. Initially resistant, we gave CPS a hard time, prompting a CPS woman named Danita Sampson to enter and loudly announce, "It's easier to cooperate and just get it over with! We're just checking for weight, height, ears, heart, lungs, no undressing, and get a picture!" They had finally caught on to our strong resistance to undergoing full physicals. Subsequently, the children began their exams, accompanied by their mothers. We spent almost the entire morning waiting for our turn. Meanwhile, the mothers met with some of our attorneys in groups throughout the morning. For some reason, Mother Annette, Aunt Barbara, and Mother Paula joined the Rangers and were absent until 2:00 pm.

My sister Shirley Allred, married to Seth Allred, and Sarah Monique Barlow, married to Jacob Barlow Jr, had been removed from the ranch, though childless and their husband's only wife. They desired to return home to the ranch and inquired of CPS the possibility of doing so. This started rumors flying that some mothers were trying to sneak off the

Fort's grounds with their children. During lunch, a state trooper named Baily barged in and exclaimed, "I want eyeball to eyeball with each one of you!" His intensity was evident as he warned us about rumors suggesting some mothers were considering leaving the shelters with their children. He threatened, "If you do that, you will be arrested, put in prison, and not allowed back here with your children!"

After this, CPS began to crowd among us more and became more watchful and attentive, attempting to listen to everything we said. They strategically positioned themselves where they could observe each one of us. When some of them who were seated under the loft took a break, my older sister Maryanne and I occupied their places and read children's books she had brought from home. Upon their return, we ignored their presence, so they stood close by.

That afternoon, I called Uncle Merril, and he advised us to be quieter and not engage with CPS at all. He stated that they were looking for any reason they could to separate mothers from their children and turning anything we said against us. We discreetly passed this message to everyone old enough to maintain silence. Meanwhile, CPS tried engaging us in conversations and eavesdropping on ours. Many of them acted amiable towards the children but kept a vigilant eye on the older kids and mothers. I started feeling a sense of impending events. Sensing I was being closely watched, I stayed close to my cot.

Chapter Eight

"We Find Things Around Here"

I tried hard to stay out of the limelight while at shelter 2. When Father sent a message to me from the Mohave County jail in Arizona to oversee the prayer times at the shelter, I obeyed. CPS monitored me closer after this.

On April 10, at 4:20 pm, I walked to the middle of the shelter for a snack. A CPS lady approached me, asking Mother Annette and me to step outside to speak. Once outside, she informed us they had decided to move me to shelter 7 where the teenage boys had been housed after being the last children to be taken from the YFZ ranch. Mother Annette questioned, "I've been trying to get my son Helaman over here. I thought you were trying to reunite families." The CPS official replied, "We have custody of him and can decide where we want him to be. We feel it's in the best interest of this shelter."

They instructed me to gather my belongings and accompany them. Two extremely obese CPS women escorted me while three police officers followed on a golf cart. We walked down a dirt road to Shelter 7. One of the women, hailing from Houston, shared her terrifying experience with the tornado storm the night before. She recounted, "When those sirens went off, me an' my blankets an' my pillows went into the tub and didn't come out until them sirens stopped!"

Upon arrival at Shelter 7, the boys, including myself, were furious about the situation. These boys were my classmates. They had hidden out in the bushes and boulder piles at home from CPS until Uncle Merril told them it would be best if they turned themselves in. Their siblings had already been removed and CPS refused to reunite them with their families, sheltering them separately. From then on, we asked every person entering our shelter to reunite us with our families until they grew exasperated. About half an hour after my arrival, they took us to their clinic for an exam. When they asked for my personal information, in my anger, I refused to disclose anything.

They weighed me on a scale and then checked my height. Next, they tested the reflex in my knee. They examined my eyes, ears, and shone a light into my mouth. Then they prodded my belly, asking if it hurt anywhere. This was the procedure they performed on each one of us. After the examination, they took our photographs.

After returning, I gathered all the boys, and we went outside to kick balls. We needed an outlet for the fury we felt. Although CPS had set boundaries on the field, we kept going past them to retrieve the balls we were kicking. CPS and the police grew uneasy about it, and two officers drove onto the field in their car, ordering us back into the shelter. They stationed officers at each door and around the building. Three sergeants came in to speak with us, clearly upset. One of them said, "If you want attention, you're going to get it, but not the way you want. You can be big. Now, we must post an officer at every door!" It dawned on me that they thought we might run away, so I clarified, "We're not going to run away. We are very close to our families, and we want to be back with them. We will cooperate, but we're still going to ask for what we want!" After my explanation, they departed. From then on, they wouldn't permit us to shower after dark, and we were required to be inside our shelter by 7:00 pm. Despite my repeated requests, CPS refused to take my laundry to get washed. I finally asked some MHMR (Mental Health Mental Retardation) volunteers to take it to be washed, which they kindly did.

A little after 7:00 pm, Jimmy Simmons, the CPS worker in charge of the shelter 7 separated the teenage boys at shelter 3 from their families and brought them to our shelter. They were: Mahonri Jeffs, Merril Jeffs,

Joshua Nielsen, Jason Musser, and Jason Dockstader. As they entered, officers immediately took their duffel bags and searched their belongings. One officer took out Josh's long underwear, and Josh said, "Don't you dare let that touch the ground!" (In the FLDS, the long undergarments are considered sacred clothing and are worn starting at about 3 years old) so the officer held them above the ground and started shaking them out. Josh quipped, "Nope, Sarah isn't in there!" Everyone laughed, and the officer, somewhat embarrassed, said, "I'm just seeing if you have knives or anything dangerous."

With 16 boys now in shelter 7, three CPS officials watched over us at night. One of them was so large that he could barely squeeze through the door sideways, and when he sat down, he occupied two chairs. (Seeing obese individuals was a new experience for us, as most in our community were slender from manual labor and a healthy diet) When they arrived, we promptly engaged in our reading and prayer before going to bed. Because it got so hot during the day, CPS had a temporary A/C unit installed. At night, we made the room as cold as possible by adjusting the AC and turning on two huge fans. By morning, all the CPS individuals in there were wrapped in blankets.

Day 9

During the daytime, Jimmy Simmons served as our CPS shelter manager. He was reasonable and allowed us our space. Our CPS watchers enjoyed sitting on the boardwalk and chatting with the police officers who were also stationed there, keeping an eye on us. We didn't have much to do in our shelter throughout the day besides working on some large puzzles and whatever games we could come up with. It was hot in the daytime, so we stayed inside until evening. When it cooled off at day's end, we'd go out and play soccer, sit in the grass breaking grass stems, or quizzing the cops about all their gear and asking them to tell us their scariest stories.

That afternoon, I went behind our shelter to the restroom trailer, only to find there were no guards watching us. As I emerged from the trailer, I realized I was alone at the back of our shelter. Usually, there were two officers nearby, but they were absent. Immediately, the thought crossed my mind to sneak away from the Fort and be done with it all. The stress of our situation weighed heavily on me, and I contemplated leaving, thinking, "You are not needed here any longer. Staying won't do any good anyway." I had seen trucks come by every day that I knew were men from home who were staying close by, hoping to get a glimpse of their families. I could easily get a ride home. However, a better thought prevailed, reminding me that I needed to stay and endure. I hurried back to where the other boys were, resolving not to entertain thoughts of running away. It was the only time I ever saw that area unguarded.

In the evening, we played a soccer game. The police officers seemed to enjoy watching and even provided us with four large traffic cones to use for our goals. Nothing noteworthy occurred for a couple of days at our shelter. We continued with our prayer times and reading. During the shift change in the evening, we all went straight to bed.

Day 10

On the morning of April 12th, Jimmy Simmons entered shelter 7 and asked if we preferred a straightforward or roundabout explanation of how things were going with CPS decision making. We opted for straightforward, to which he replied, "It's the same *shit,* just another day. I am just as frustrated as you guys. It's like the blind are leading the blind." Jimmy was an excellent tobacco chewer, displaying perfect aim when spitting. We found it quite unusual.

In the afternoon, we sang outside for a while before sitting on the grass. We engaged in a game to find the strongest piece of grass, which occupied us for hours due to a lack of other activities. In the evening, we played soccer once more. I finally managed to get my laundry done so I could have a shower. Prior to my stay at Shelter 7, I had only showered once at Shelter 2, and it had been a week since then. The showers at shelter 2 were in a large trailer, with three or four shower heads on the wall and only shower curtains for privacy. This made for a very precarious undertaking, because of our rules on modesty. The showers at shelter 7 were in a trailer, each separated from the other, with one on each of the three corners and the restroom on the fourth corner. If more than one boy was showering, they would surprise each other by jumping on their corner of the trailer to launch the other boy up into the air during his shower.

Day 11

On Sunday the 13th, we had Sunday School, reading from the little book called "Government of God" and the "Doctrine and Covenants." Later, we noticed news reporters across from us at Fort Concho trying to get our attention, so we lined up on the boardwalk for a picture. I called some of my sisters in shelter two and learned that one or two of the mothers there had talked to the news media about conditions in the shelters and how CPS had been treating them. The repercussions came shortly afterward, and soon Maryanne informed me that a large group of state troopers were taking away all the phones. Nearly all of us boys had cell phones. I alerted the boys, and we swiftly hid our phones in various locations on top of the rock walls in the shelter. We all thought that was an excellent hiding spot, but I felt a prompting to move mine. I hid my phone as far back as I could in the metal duct where the AC was blowing, praying to God to keep it hidden when they came. We waited on the boardwalk to see when they would come.

The officers were taking their time searching the other shelters, so the day dragged on slowly as we waited and waited. Later that morning, CPS brought 11 more boys to our shelter from the Pavilion, totaling 27 boys. Among them were my brothers Helaman, Raymond, Richard, and David. They seemed quite shaken from the separation they had experienced. It was comforting to see them, and they were glad to be reunited with us. It struck us as odd, though, that they had brought these boys over, as Jimmy Simmons had previously informed us that CPS intended to move everyone to the Coliseum. However, we had learned not to trust everything they told us.

Upon the arrival of these boys, we engaged in our usual game of finding the strongest piece of grass on the field. At 1:00 pm, we observed about ten DPS officers approaching, and we went to meet them. Officer Speed gathered us in our shelter and showed us a court order signed by Judge Barbara Walther, allowing them to confiscate our phones "or any communication device which may interfere with the investigation." They requested us to voluntarily surrender our phones. Several boys had already been searched by this same officer when taken from home and had given him non-functional phones while hiding their working phone in their shoes. They informed him, "You already took our phones."

Subsequently, they used metal detectors to search us and instructed us to go outside and wait. Before all of us were outside, they found the first phone, which sparked their suspicion that more phones were hidden. Consequently, they extensively searched the building with metal detectors, locating all the phones on top the rock walls and one inside a cavity in another wall.

I witnessed an officer cooling off by the AC reach his arm all the way in, presumably to check for hidden phones. If he had been attentive, he would have struck gold. The color drained from my face, and my knees nearly buckled. I felt sick and had to sit down on the boardwalk. I pled with God to let us keep at least one phone so we could keep a line of communication with our parents and inform them of CPS' actions.

Officer Speed grew displeased as they discovered phone after phone and reprimanded us for not willingly surrendering the phones. He accused us of committing a sin of omission by withholding them. We laughed in response, and Mitchel remarked, "You didn't do a good enough search the first time." Our families in the other shelters had turned most of their phones in because of the threats that any mother found with one would be removed from her children, and very few kept a phone hidden. We were the first shelter where the officers had met resistance. They knew we had somehow been informed and purposely hid our phones instead of turning them in.

The officers rummaged through the garbage can and then approached the large ice chest where we stored our juice. The staff also used it to keep their soda pop and Coke. They questioned Mormon Allred, "Are there any phones in here?" He replied, "What if I said no?" Without delay, they delved in, exploring the freezing ice water for hidden phones. We had just shaken up the bottles of Coke as a joke on the staff. Some of the officers asked if they could have a drink. I told them it was going to be a sticky mess, but they ignored me until they opened the Coke, and it blew everywhere, to our amusement. When the officers departed, one of them remarked, "We find things around here."

In their frustration, they also confiscated all the phone chargers except Merril's. When no one was looking, I reached inside the duct and, to my immense relief, my phone was still there! I was grateful for long arms and knowing that some sins of omission could be beneficial. I concealed my phone and refrained from turning it on for a couple of days afterward.

After the officers left, we resumed reading from the scriptures. An hour later, two CASA (Court Appointed Special Advocate) workers individually conversed with each of us. The worker who spoke to me mentioned they would convey our desires to the judge. I expressed our longing to go home, and she revealed that was the unanimous sentiment of all the children. At first, we thought CASA was our friend, but after several weeks, I concluded that CASA workers advocate for their program rather than prioritizing the children's best interests.

From 2:45 to 4:20 pm, we went outside and sang hymns to our families in the other shelters. Initially restricted by CPS from going beyond the first light plant eastward, we eventually obtained permission to sing near the flagpole. We sang "You Can Make the Pathway Bright" and "Redeemer of Israel." Following our songs, our families responded with their own. The people in shelters 1 and 2 sang "Shall the Youth of Zion Falter?" and those in shelter three sang "God be With You." Subsequently, we went inside for dinner.

During the weekend staff change, we encountered a few CPS officials who were more considerate than many we had previously interacted with. They told us lots of fun stories about their adventures, building up quite a rapport with us. We had a good time with them. Since getting CPS to provide anything for us was challenging, we waited for an MHMR (Mental Health Mental Retardation) worker named Eddie Wallace and his assistants to check on us and then request what we needed. We would ask for snacks, balls, puzzles, and other activities. We always asked them to take care of our laundry. They were kind and provided for us. Each day, several BCFS workers and one or two doctors visited us. Additionally, CPS asked for our names and dates of birth at least once a day.

Chapter Nine

Betrayal

Day 12

We awoke on Monday, April 14 with great hopes that we would get to return home this week. CPS interviews were over, and it felt like we were just biding our time, waiting for a decision by those in charge of CPS. We did not understand all the ramifications of our removal and the court hearings that would be required before we would get to return home.

At 10:00 am, a CPS woman arrived at our shelter and informed us she had an announcement to make. We all gathered around her in hopeful anticipation that everything would start changing for the better. She delivered a brief message from a piece of paper she held stating that all people in the shelters would be relocated to a single place for family reunification and better facilitation. She declined to disclose the location, leaving us with mixed feelings. "Should we trust them for once or is it just another lie?" we wondered. Jimmy Simmons and other CPS and DPS officials had mentioned, during the previous week, that those in charge had decided to move everyone from Fort Concho to the Coliseum in San Angelo. We ardently hoped it would be so.

We packed our few belongings and prepared to leave. Concerned about being searched, I hid my phone in my thickest pair of socks and placed it in my brother Helaman's bag. He was younger and would not be punished if he were found with it.

Jimmy Simmons had left for the weekend and told us he would be back Monday. When he did not show, we inquired about his whereabouts. His coworkers told us his wife was in an accident and he had been called home. This made us suspicious. Randy Shell, another CPS official, informed us he would be taking charge of us now. He told us he would return in an hour after preparing for the trip. This got me wondering why he needed an hour if we were just moving across the city, and I began to question if they were telling the truth.

Upon Randy Shell's return, he requested we choose a group leader, and I was nominated due to being the oldest. As he lined us up and read our names, it became apparent that this relocation might be more complex than initially presented. Many buses were pulling in at the various shelters at Fort Concho. They all said "Red Carpet" on them. Boarding a Red Carpet bus, we were joined by CPS workers (who had formerly been law enforcement officers), DPS officers, an MHMR worker, and medical personnel. The situation grew more suspicious as Randy Shell performed a roll call and required anyone with any medication to get it out of their bags in the cargo bay and have it with them on the bus. By now, I really wondered how much we were being lied to in this operation.

As the bus was about to depart, Randy Shell addressed us on the bus mic. He announced that we needed to be ready for six or seven hours of travel. Everyone else would be going to the San Angelo Coliseum, but we would be going to a place called Cal Farley's Boys Ranch near Amarillo, in the panhandle of Texas. The shock and anger among the boys were palpable. We felt betrayed, especially with the promise of being reunited with our families that was made a few hours earlier.

As Randy saw the look on the boys' faces turn to extreme frustration, he quickly added that this place was almost like our home, and it would be a fun place for us. He said they had brought snacks and a meal for us. At this point, I looked back at the other boys and saw written on their faces extreme frustration, hot indignation, and stupefied astonishment. This was so distant from anything we had expected that we were dumbfounded. Some of the youngest put their heads down and cried, while others looked ready to fight it out right there. And the officers looked ready for it. As I contemplated this scene for a moment, all the boys looking at me as if I should speak, the words came out of my mouth as quick as the thought came into my mind, and I whispered, "Let's just be at peace." I won't say we felt any sudden relief, but the tension started to clear a little and we settled down. But we were still very angry. We had never felt so betrayed. The anger in this moment inspired me to begin looking for a means of escape for all of us.

Randy Shell sat down, and the bus pulled out. An extra bus and an ambulance followed behind. We were escorted by four State Trooper cars. Just before leaving the city of San Angelo, the buses stopped at the gas station and fueled. There was hushed whispering among the boys as several of them considered opening the emergency exit windows and jumping out, but cooler tempers prevailed. As we drove through the city, law enforcement blocked off every intersection so we could drive right through. It was quite the parade. As we traveled along, we sang three songs to help us cope with the situation, but after that, we felt too sad and cross to sing anymore. I watched Randy Shell and another CPS worker talking. The other worker laughingly pointed up at something on the shelf of the bus and asked Randy if he knew what it was. Randy said he did, and they both laughed. I studied what was on the shelf for a minute when I realized the "object" they were talking about was a bunch of zip-tie handcuffs. I was very grateful we had kept at peace instead of having a row.

During the trip, I went to the restroom located at the back of the bus. On my way back to my seat, I stopped to talk to Sam Jessop. He told me, "The maddest I have ever felt in my whole life was today when they tricked us onto the bus and yesterday when they took our phones!" I agreed.

The distance from San Angelo to Boys Ranch is 350 miles, 403 miles from home. As we were traveling, Randy Shell asked us if we wanted to have TVs and radios in the house they were taking us to. Everyone shouted, "NO!" This was something we were taught was evil to have. We were told this is how the devil got evil into our minds. He said he would make sure they were removed before we arrived there. Late in the afternoon, Randy Shell got the meal out that they had brought along, but no one felt like eating.

At 6:15 pm, we drove into Amarillo. We were told we had 45 more minutes of travel left. As we traveled, we took careful note of which roads we went on. We finally drove into Cal Farley's Boys Ranch at 7:00 pm. This was a devastating blow to us to be taken so far from home and those we loved. As we were traveling, I wrote in my little notebook:

"At 12:00, we were loaded on the bus and were told that everyone else was going to the Coliseum, but that they were taking all of us boys to a ranch house up by Amarillo. It was quite shocking, to say it mildly. The Lord will bring us home. He is our only strength in this hour of great need. We have one Hwy Patrol in front, 1 extra bus behind with 3 more patrols, and an ambulance also."

The buses pulled into Boys Ranch and took us over to the dining hall. We unloaded off the bus and went inside. The staff there had kindly prepared a meal for us. They tried to welcome us and make us feel comfortable, but it didn't work. We were still mad, feeling betrayed, and no one wanted to eat. Randy Shell finally convinced us to do so. We all dished up a little food and sat down at the tables to eat. My appetite was gone, and the food was tasteless to me. While we were sitting there, a Boys Ranch staff came up to Johnny Jessop, one of my high school friends, and asked, "Is there something I can do for you?" He demanded, "Let me borrow your phone for a minute." They said, "I'm sorry, I can't let you do that." And he replied, "Well, then get out of here!!" Johnny always did well at expressing the anger we all felt.

A couple of the younger boys needed to go to the restroom, so I walked with them to the restrooms in the building. To my utmost surprise, there were no doors on the bathroom stalls. These kinds of things were a complete culture shock to us. They begged me to stand guard at the restroom entrance while each one of them took their turn, so no one would walk in on them. As soon as we were finished eating, we boarded back on the bus and were driven up to our new living quarters.

Chapter Ten

Cal Farley's Boys Ranch

C al Farley's Boys Ranch is a small community devoted to helping boys and girls become responsible and resilient adults. The ranch was started in 1939 by a man named Cal Farley, who was a professional wrestler and businessman. It is located 36 miles northwest of Amarillo, Texas, on the Canadian River. It is an oasis in the desert. Boys Ranch is on the former site of an old western cattle town called Old Tascosa. There was a chapel and a public school system with grades K-12. The ranch had a large gym, racetrack, football field, rodeo arena, housing for the nearly 400 children there, and housing for many of the staff and their families. The staff told us the piece of land where the community is located is between 1200 and 1300 acres. In size comparison, the YFZ ranch was about 1700 acres.

After serving us dinner, Boys Ranch staff escorted us to a house called the "Hamilton House." They informed us this was our home for now. We unloaded our belongings and gathered into the living room. The Boys Ranch staff could tell by our looks and actions that we were angry about being there and tried to help us calm down. They were kind and asked us what food was acceptable in our culture. They also wanted to accommodate us with the same schedule as we were used to at home. I asked them to give us privacy in our prayer and reading times as much as their rules would allow. They courteously agreed to this. Later, several of the staff enjoyed being part of our prayer times.

We were shown to our rooms, and to our amazement, there were no doors on the bedrooms. The bathrooms also had no doors. Inside the bathroom were two toilets and a urinal side by side with no partition between them. In the shower compartment, there were two shower heads sticking out of the wall instead of two shower stalls. We had lived a life of privacy in these matters. We were quite disappointed and demanded them to get us something for privacy. I guess we must've seemed quite angry because we got those staff members on their toes, rushing around to find whatever they could to make us happy. They quickly gathered up a bunch of sheets and gray tape for us. We taped the sheets up and used them for our temporary doors. They told us they would get us shower curtains the next day.

When we went to the restroom, we learned quick to shout before entering, "Is anybody in here?" And we did a lot of singing and whistling when in the restroom to alert others when we were in there.

The house had a large living room on the south with a kitchen straight across the hall from it. On the west side of the kitchen were two bedrooms, and on the east were three more. There was one long hall that went from one side of the house to the other, with an outside door on each end. All our bedrooms were on the north side of the hall. Adjacent to each side of the living room were the staff quarters, where they had a couple of bedrooms, an office, and a laundry room. We also had a laundry area on the south side of the hall with one washer and dryer.

We had our prayer and reading and began to get settled into the house. It was amazing to me at the time to have a real bed again and to be able to go into a room without someone sitting right there, watching me. The only place with a door was our closets, which were so small that a person could barely fit inside.

After everyone was settled and getting to bed, I got my phone out of Helaman's bag and went into the closet to make some calls. I had not turned it on since we were searched for phones, and none of our parents knew where we had been taken. I first called Mother Naomie, who was staying in Kingman, Arizona and told her where we were. She would be able to inform my Father, who was in Kingman jail, what was taking place. She asked, "What in the world are you doing clear up there?" She then told me the awful story of what had happened that day in the separating of the mothers from the children at the Pavilion, which kindled up more feelings of sorrow and anger within me. I wondered if I could take any more. Ever since we started for Boys Ranch, I had been thinking, "At least the other children who were separated are now reunited with their mothers and siblings." I was extremely disappointed again and dreadfully worried about my other siblings.

After this, I called Uncle Merril and many of the parents of the boys to inform them where we were. All of them were shocked to learn we had been taken so far away from home. I was extremely careful with the phone, as most of the boys with me still didn't know I had been able to get mine through the search.

Day 13

The next day, I noted this down in my little notebook:

"On the 14th, the CPS people asked all the mothers [at the pavilion] to come in a different room without the children. In that room were 80 police. They read something to them that said they had no more parental rights over their children and that the children were in full state custody. They were offered to go to a 'battered woman's shelter' where they might receive their children sooner, but then they were refused even that and were forced from their children and taken back home. Only those with children under 5 years remained, and that group, with their young ones, was separated from the children between 5 and 17. All of the children were taken to the Coliseum."

I didn't understand at first that the Wells Fargo Pavilion was a separate building from the San Angelo Coliseum. Mothers with children under five years of age remained with their children and were taken to the Coliseum. Mothers without children under five years of age were separated from all their children at the Pavilion.

The boys who were sent to Boys Ranch that day were: Ammon Jeffs, Brandon Steed, Leslie Steed, Mitchel Jeffs, Mormon Allred, Ammon Steed, Steven Dockstader, Sampson Jessop, Johnson Jessop, Merril Jeffs, Joshua Nielsen, Levi Steed, Jeremiah Keate, Jason Dockstader, Helaman Jeffs, Raymond Jeffs, Richard Jeffs, David Jeffs, Mahonri Jeffs, Curtis Jeffs, James Jeffs, Ephraim Jessop, Samuel Jeffs, Edward Barlow, Warren Dockstader, Daniel Jessop, and Jason Musser—27 total, and ages ranged from twelve to seventeen years.

The next day we arose around 6:00 am and had prayer and reading. Tim Job and a few of the staff prepared our breakfast. They cooked a large pot of oatmeal, but it was their first try at cooking it like that, and it turned into thick glue. We didn't eat hardly any of it. Then, they made eggs and bacon instead, which were delicious. The manager of the ranch, Mark Strother, wanted us to go on a tour of the place. We all boarded one of their buses and were taken all around the ranch.

One of the first orders of business after the tour was to figure out how to charge my phone. Merril was the only boy who didn't get his phone charger taken, but it did not fit my phone. Mormon cut the end of it off and stripped the wires. We tried taping them to the battery, but it did not work. After working on it for an hour and trying many things, I finally smashed the wires against the battery in the phone, and to my intense relief, it started charging.

At first, the staff would scarcely let us go outside at all. They would gather us together in the living room every few hours and do a headcount. They questioned us continually about our religion. They wanted to know everything. We felt like curiosities. They also walked in and out of our rooms freely. This bothered us, and we pressured them to give us our privacy.

After lunch, they asked if we would like to go on a hike to a place they called "the end of the world." We gladly consented, and most of us went. We walked from our house down a dirt road for quite a ways, went under the highway, and then got on a trail. It took us to a point on the Canadian River where there was a forty-foot cliff. We threw rocks off for a little bit. Until then, we had stayed right with the staff. But on the way back, we all ran! Most of us left the trail to take our own shortcut back towards the highway where the dirt road went under the bridge. We were all over the hills out there, and it suddenly dawned on me that the staff were trying their utmost to stay with us lest we run away. It was hilarious to watch them running to catch up to a group of boys, only to find another group way off somewhere else and then go running after them. Anyhow, we all made it safely back to our house. The staff were clearly worn out, and they were sure to let us know that we needed to stay together with them next time "for our safety!"

When we got back, we found Ammon Steed and Merril Jeffs busily engaged in teaching the gospel to some of the Boys Ranch staff and CPS workers. When I walked in the door, there was a stack of novels sitting on the table. Novels were strictly forbidden at home, so I asked Randy

Shell, "What are these doing here? Aren't these novels?" He said, "Those are good books. You can learn a good lesson from fables." I said, "But they're not the truth, and we want them out." He removed them.

When we arrived at the ranch, another CPS worker from Wichita Falls had been sent there to be with us for a week. He had not been involved with the case before this. After we told him what we had been through and how much we hated CPS, he took his name card off and begged us to treat him like he was our friend and not even think of him as a CPS worker while he was there. He was kind and considerate, and we got along well with him. Another kind CPS worker named Juan Martinez came with us from San Angelo and stayed a week. He later became Mother Annette's caseworker. He was Hispanic and was chubby, something novel to us. He always told us he had eaten too many burritos.

After this, the staff gathered us and discussed what we should do each day. They told me they would like us to split up into small groups and work in different areas of the ranch with their professionals of different trades. I told them I'd think about it. After that, we older boys discussed the subject together. We remembered the counsel our parents had given us to stay together as much as possible. After the experiences of having first been taken from home, then separated from our families, and finally, in a surprise move, transported hundreds of miles from home, we were unwilling to make it easy to separate ourselves now. We were extremely distrustful of the staff after having been deceived and lied to the past two weeks by CPS. After dinner, the staff gathered us together again and asked me what I thought. I simply said, "No, we will stay together." I noted this down at the time:

"They gave me all of their reasons and even offered money [for the work we would do], but it changeth not my mind. We will stick together after all the lying and outrageous things and moves they have done, even being 'kidnapped' by the state and put about 500 miles from our home."

They brought us a large amount of shower curtains, and we hung them up in our bedroom and bathroom doorways. Some of the curtains had a clear part, so they could still look in our rooms.

That evening, several of us boys went on a walk with CPS worker Randy Shell from our house down to the rodeo arena. We didn't check in with the staff before we left. They became worried and went looking all over the ranch for us. They found us just as we were heading back to the house. One of them, Leon Hollice, told me it was very dangerous for us to go without them, as some of the other boys who resided at the ranch might try saying or doing something to harm us. I told him I knew how to protect myself if I needed to. He said, "Well, you boys don't know how to defend yourselves if someone tries hurting you." I didn't reply and kept my peace. They had us climb in Kraig Stockstill's truck and ride back up to the house.

When we were getting ready to go to bed, Randy Shell told us we needed to wear pajamas at night. He had some there for us. We asked him what they looked like. He held a pair up and said, "They're shorts!" This was impermissible in our culture. We always wore long sleeves and pants. Even our night clothes were long sleeved tops and full-length bottoms. Doing otherwise was considered sinful exposure of our bodies. None of us had brought our pajamas. We told him we would be fine sleeping in our day clothes. Our staff kept up a night watch. They were loud and boisterous in the living room until well past midnight.

Day 14

The next day, they let us go outside more. We asked them about planting a garden. They told us they would look for a place to do it close to our house, but nothing ever came of it. Mid-morning, a group of us went down to the clinic for a checkup. Tommy Brian, a Registered Nurse, was the boss there. He looked over the records sent by CPS about us and did basic checkups on us.

Chapter Eleven

We Have to Stay

T he date for our first court hearing was April 16. Several of our attorneys came to talk to us before this Adversary Hearing. My attorney, Kevin Isern, was unable to come, so he asked another attorney in his firm, Gregg Freeman to talk to his clients. Gregg Freeman told us our rights and let us write a letter to the judge. He told us he would try to get our letters to her, but he didn't know if he would be able to. Our letters never reached her. We wrote them in great anger with caustic and offensive language. In the afternoon, a big storm blew in. Our staff wouldn't let us step out the door, even though our custom at home was to go outside and watch the storms.

The staff was having a hard time identifying us, so they made us name cards to wear. We also wanted to be able to use them later as ID cards for getting our drivers licenses. We wore them for a couple of days until the staff got to know us.

That afternoon, Mark Strother, manager of the ranch, took us down to ranch headquarters and showed us a news clip where some of our mothers talked to the news reporters. It was the first time we saw any media coverage of the raid. We all were glad to finally see what was being said about it in public. Although watching the news was not allowed at home, we felt justified because our parents were being filmed.

When I came back up to the house that evening, Ammon Steed had just finished reading LDS church founder Joseph Smith's first vision to some of the staff and CPS workers. One of the CPS workers, Clarence D. Holditch, an older man, said to me, "If there is light, what is it? I am so confused." Apparently, Ammon Steed's discussion about Joseph Smith founding the LDS church left him very perplexed about religion. He was leaving that night, and he gave all of us his phone number. Unfortunately, I lost his number before leaving Boys Ranch. One thing I remember about Clarence: My first night in Shelter 7 was very cold because all I had was a thin blanket CPS had provided me with. Sometime late in the night, I woke up and realized there was a sleeping bag covering me, and I wasn't cold anymore. The next morning, after we arose, he told us that he was checking on us during the night and saw one of us shivering with cold, so he put a sleeping bag over him. I have always felt grateful to him for that act of kindness.

Several of the boys' parents brought duffel bags of clothes to the ranch after we had been there a few days. They informed me that there would be more phones hidden in the clothes and to be very careful when they brought the bags to search them. Boys Ranch staff let us come down to headquarters to get the bags of clothes. They were supposed to search them with us and inventory everything that came. We quickly found the phones in a few pairs of socks and hid them before the staff could see them.

That night, attorney Vincent Nowak came to talk to his clients, my brothers Ray, Rich, and cousin Mahonri. He was very kind and asked us to explain a summary of our religion to him. While we were talking with him, Randy Shell and all the other CPS workers besides Juan Martinez left. We were grateful for that and felt safer without them.

Day 15

April 17 was a cloudy, cold, windy day. Our staff brought us all warm jackets. They let a few of us go outside without being right by them. Mahonri and I ran up the hill that was by our house and had a good look around. We could see most of Boys Ranch and a line of windmills on the horizon. He took a few pictures of the place while we were up there.

My stepbrother David wrote a little note to Mark Strother, the manager of the ranch, asking him to go to Warren Cat in San Angelo and get him a hat with pictures of big equipment on it. David loved big equipment. There were two DPS officers coming to check on us, so they got David a hat at the Cat dealership in Amarillo and brought two boxes of hats for everyone else. We thought this to be very kind of them.

The Adversary Hearing for all 416 of the children taken from the ranch began, and we hoped for a miracle, although our attorneys said the odds were stacked against our release. It was the largest child custody case in U.S. history.

Day 16

On April 18, the court hearing in San Angelo continued. The younger boys went to the clinic to get a check-up, and they asked me to go with them. Justin Ford, a Boys Ranch staff took us down there. At one point, for some reason, I was the only one out in the hall with him. While out there, he asked me why I acted afraid to answer his questions a few days before when he entered my room, opened my Book of Mormon, and started asking questions. I told him I was not afraid but felt uncomfortable with his sense of entitlement to come touch my belongings without my permission. He asked me, "Do you think it is okay to lie."

"No, I haven't been taught that way."

"What about Moses in the Bible when his mother lied about him? Does that mean it's okay to lie?"

"No, that doesn't make it okay to lie."

"Does that mean Moses' mother was doing wrong?"

"What would you do if your child was going to be killed? Would you lie if you knew he would be saved?"

"Probably so, but does that mean it's okay or good to lie?"

"That's not what I understand it to mean."

Several of the staff had similar conversations with the other boys, and I was confused about why our staff wanted to twist us in our words and make us admit lying was okay if it was to protect our parents. Why were they interrogating us like CPS?

Late that morning, I borrowed a pair of binoculars from one of the other boys and went up on the hill by our house. I wanted to get a good look at the windmills I had seen the day previous and get a better look around the region. I guess the staff saw me, and it made them agitated. Later in the day, Ben Carpenter, a Boys Ranch staff, came to me and told me that no one had ever escaped from Boys Ranch. He said one boy tried it and had frozen to death in the night. He also told me that when boys would run away, they would park their truck in a dip up on the hill, and when the boy would come by, they would shine their lights on him and surprise him. I didn't know why he was telling me all of this, so I just was saying, "Huh, pretty amazing" and such.

That evening as we gathered for prayer and reading, the staff called me into their quarters alone. They had me sit down between two large men with another man facing me. I felt small and slim right there. One of them, named Chris, started speaking. He told me, "We have a boy here who had a friend that just died. That boy is going to have to somehow let his sorrow out because it is like trying to hold a balloon underwater;

it is going to pop up somewhere. If he doesn't let it out by crying, he is going to do something else to let it out, like get angry or something of that nature. He has to let it out somehow." Leon Hollice added, "Big men don't cry."

I sat there completely bewildered as to why they were telling me about someone else's problem. It dawned on me after a few minutes of talking when Chris suddenly asked, "Why did you go running up the hill today?" So, this was about me, not the other boy. I wondered why on earth it mattered if I did or not. I had been up there several times the day before just for something to do. I thought up a reason fast, "When I was young, I lived in the mountains and loved to climb. I just wanted to climb up something." They asked, "Aren't you worried about what is going to happen in this court hearing, though?" I remembered hearing whisperings among staff and others wondering if we would harm ourselves if everything didn't turn out how we desired, so I looked him straight in the eye and replied, "Not at all." This caught them off guard, and they dropped the subject. Leon Hollice told me we needed to mingle with the staff more and not isolate ourselves. He told me I needed to come to them and discuss my emotions. Of course, I became more determined to keep my current course, as we believed everyone was trying to turn us from our faith. At the same time, all 26 of the other boys sat in silence and worry, wondering what tricks were going to be played on us next.

Leon told me they were very impressed when we entered the house and removed our shoes the first day we came. He also asked that we remove our hats when in the house to honor its dedication. I acquiesced. He requested I write up a list of our "unwritten rules" and meet with him again, and he would have his list of theirs. After talking to me and questioning me from about 6:55 until 7:20 pm, they let me out. When I came back into the living room with the other boys, I felt flushed and sick, but told them everything was going to be fine. I had been terrified when going in there that another separation was about to happen.

A little while after our prayer time, Mark Strother, the ranch manager, and Juan Martinez, a CPS worker, came to tell us the decision of the court. Mark announced to us that Judge Walther had made the decision to keep us in state custody. All our hopes of going home were dashed. We had to stay.

After Mark informed us of the court's decision, we asked many questions about how long we would be kept from home. Juan Martinez could tell we were extremely disappointed with the court's decision. He said, "You need to realize it's not your fault that this has happened. It's not your fault," inferring that it was the fault of our parents. That made us angry, and we became defensive of our parents. Juan apologized, and they left. We all felt terribly despondent, so we gathered in one of the bedrooms, sang a hymn, and talked together, consoling each other. We had hoped for days that at this hearing, the judge would see CPS' error in removing us and return us home. For a while it felt like we were living in a daze. None of us had expected to be gone for long. We couldn't believe this was happening to us. We understood we might end up being in state custody for many months now. We now put our hope in the next hearings that were to take place within 60 days of our removal.

Chapter Twelve

Overwhelmed

Day 17

On April 19, Mark Strother asked me if we would like to have more boys join us from the shelters in San Angelo. I told him I would consider it and let him know. That evening, we discussed it among ourselves and concluded if CPS were going to separate the children in San Angelo into small groups and spread them across the state like us, we wanted as many as possible to live with us. When Mark came and asked me again, I told him, "Yes, if they won't let everyone stay together, we would like all the boys to come here." Mr. Strother told me that CPS had asked if they could send the boys from the Pavilion up to Boys Ranch, and he would tell them we would take them.

The staff brought us a bunch of lariats and a calf roping dummy, so we could learn how to rope. Many of the boys became apt at this skill while we were at Boys Ranch. Sometimes, in the evening, two rows of boys with lariats would line up, and we would run between them to see if they could rope us. It proved to be cruel exercise with rope burns on our necks, arms, and legs. When the younger boys came, we stopped roping each other.

Up until now, I had been jamming the wires from Merril's charger against the battery in my phone to charge it. I needed a phone charger. I secretly called Wendell Nielsen, the First Counselor in the First Presidency of the FLDS church, who told me he would be passing by Boy's Ranch in a few days with his son Rich. They would be able to work something out. I talked to Rich Nielsen and told him what kind of phone I had. He figured out what kind of charger to get. He informed me he would be going by at about 7 am and wondered where to place it. At first, they both wanted to meet me, but I told them there was a high risk of being caught. I told him of the place where a dirt road goes under the highway on the ranch. There was a white fence post he could place it on, wrapped up in a grocery bag. I told him we would resolve it from there.

Day 18

On the morning of April 20, Wendell Nielsen passed by Boys Ranch. I called his son Rich to ensure he had dropped off the charger according to my directions. Now it was time to find a discreet way to obtain it.

We older boys discussed our options, and finally concluded to ask the staff if we could go on a walk past the highway for some exercise. They acquiesced, and early in the afternoon, we went on our walk. I arranged for the main group of boys to stay back and captivate the staff in a talk on religion while Merril and I got rowdy and ran a ways ahead of them. This plan worked well. We reached the fence post, and I snatched the grocery bag, discreetly stuffed it in my pocket, and then kept walking like nothing had happened. We were able to do it so the other boys could not tell we had gotten anything. When we turned around to go back to the house, several of the boys who understood the real purpose of our walk came running up to me and asked how we were going to get the charger. I patted my pocket, and they understood.

A man named Terry Cooper, a Boys Ranch employee, came up from the pavilion in San Angelo. He had been a volunteer since the 6th of April when we were taken to Fort Concho. This was a surprise to me, as I didn't realize Boys Ranch had volunteer staff down there. I recognized him and remembered him sitting by the fence where we would all stand and wave at family and friends in other shelters. We would kick balls over shelter 2 into the field for him to gather up until he got tired of chasing after them. All this time I had thought he was CPS. Mark Strother placed Mr. Cooper over the staff in both of our houses because he had been around our people longer and was more understanding than the other staff. Mr. Cooper told us that there would be 27 more boys coming up there.

That day, we were allowed to look at the news at headquarters again and watch some clips of the mothers talking about being separated from their children. CPS was taking a long time getting any visits or calls with our parents arranged. This was the only way we could see them. We also saw a news clip of the Catholic Pope Benedict XVI visiting the United States. This was a novelty to us, and the boys often mimicked the Pope for fun afterwards.

We became weary of staff doing night watch and checking on us often through the night. A few days after moving in, we talked to them about it. We said, "How come you guys do night watch? Of course, we're not going to run away. If we did, there is nowhere for us to go. We are out here in the middle of nowhere in the desert a long way from any big city." They agreed with us and decided to not do night watch anymore. After this, they had a staff change at 10:00 pm and usually retired to their quarters by midnight. We asked them to stop entering our bedrooms without our permission. They told us they would honor that, but Mr. Cooper said he would reserve the right to come in if he felt a need to.

With 27 more boys coming, the management of Boys Ranch decided to open another house for us. They decided to open the house directly east of Hamilton House for us to use and asked us to help them clean it out. Several of the boys went up there to help and found there were many small statues on a large glass bookshelf and many "gentile" pictures on the wall. These were pictures of the different groups of boys and girls doing activities at the ranch. We had been taught any pictures of people not fully dressed from wrist to ankle were evil to have. We were not to have pictures of anyone not part of the FLDS church.

The boys remembered the story of Abraham from the book of Jasher destroying his father's idols. Father had strongly taught us against having any type of sculpture or statue. So, Abraham-like, they started breaking the statues and pictures and throwing them in the trash. I arrived there while they were having great fun doing this. They thought they were doing a righteous thing, but it was very offensive to the staff. I realized the boys were even destroying trophies from the glass display in the house. Most of the boys had no idea what a trophy was. The staff asked me to have it stop and take everyone back to our house.

Day 19

On April 21, I turned 18 years old.

That day, we were told we would be using the house directly west, called "Tunnel Home," instead of the house to the east. The staff cleaned out Tunnel Home. We were grateful to use Tunnel, as it was closer to Hamilton than the other house and gave us better access to the fishing ponds. Mark and Terry confirmed to me that there would be 27 boys coming from the Pavilion the next day and 18 more from the Coliseum a few days later.

Late that morning, Juan Martinez brought me a paper to sign, which said I was willing to stay in state custody. I wondered if I could do more off the ranch to help the children be reunited with their parents. I discussed the situation with the older boys, who all wanted me to stay. After careful consideration, I realized the younger boys were going to be more comfortable and happier if I chose to stay, so I signed the paper. I knew I couldn't abandon them. A little later, Mark Strother brought me a paper to sign, which stated I was willing to remain at Cal Farley's Boys Ranch and abide by the rules while there. I also signed it. I was determined to stay with my younger brothers and friends until we were released from state custody.

At dinner, the staff brought me three cakes for my birthday. Two of them were chocolate, and one was M&M cookie dough. They were loaded with sugar, so I did not taste any of them, as we were not used to this kind of food at all and thought it sinful to partake of. In the spring of 2005, Father had told us God now required us to stop partaking of processed foods, cakes, and candies. Everything was to be homemade. Only after many inquiries did he allow organic sugar to be used sparingly. White sugar and white flour were out.

The boys assigned to live in Tunnel Home moved over there that night. Although we were busy preparing for more boys to come, Leon Hollice, a Boys Ranch staff who was one of our main supervisors, had been pressing me to write a list of our "unwritten rules" and have a discussion with him on them. I wasn't familiar with the term "unwritten rules," and wasn't sure what to write, so I had prepared several quotes of scripture to read him. When we finally sat at the table together, Terry Cooper, our new staff manager, showed up and inquired what we were doing. Leon Hollice told Terry we were going to discuss our unwritten rules. Terry told him that was unimportant at the present and sent him to Tunnel Home to manage the staff there. We never had the discussion. I often wondered if we could have averted much of the friction we had later with staff if we'd had the discussion.

Day 20

The morning of the April 22 was spent preparing for the younger boys to come. The oldest boys gathered with me and discussed how we would watch over and care for the younger boys. We decided that I would assign each of the younger boys to an older boy whom they would check in with through the day. In the evenings, the older boys who were assigned over the younger ones would read to them and put them to bed. We were determined to take care of all their needs.

That afternoon, they brought 36 new bunk beds and new couches for each house. We had a busy day setting up all the beds. Afterwards, I assigned an older boy to manage each room. It was kind of the managers of Boys Ranch to get all this new furniture for us.

Late that afternoon, Terry Cooper called me aside and told me the boys that were coming had been through a terrible experience in being separated from their siblings in the Pavilion that day. He said they had been so traumatized that he didn't think they would have any confidence in us when arrived here. I told him I was sure they would be glad to see us and would have confidence in us.

That evening, two state troopers came in advance of the boys that were coming. One of them had many years of experience while his coworker was a rookie. The older officer let us look in his car and hold his big rifle. He opened the trunk of his car, showed us all his gear, and told us cop stories for a while.

At 6:45 pm, the 27 boys from the Pavilion arrived. They were brought in a manner much like we were, with an extra bus, two ambulances, and four state trooper cars to escort them. Eddie Wallace, the MHMR worker, also came with them, and we were glad to see him again. The boys were called off the bus one by one by a CPS worker. We felt angry as we watched how coarsely they were treated as they disembarked from the bus. CPS treated them more like cattle than children. As each boy alighted from the bus, we greeted them, and they were extremely glad to see us. All these boys were younger than the first group of us that had come to Boys Ranch. They were wild and independent. The effects of being without their parents and fending for themselves for a week were obvious. They were extremely rude to everyone at first, especially the Boys Ranch staff.

The names of the boys who arrived were: Abraham Jeffs, Allen Jeffs, Isaac Jeffs, Jacob Jeffs, Joseph Jeffs, Josiah Jeffs, Kendall Jeffs, Matthew Jeffs, Nephi Jeffs, Royce Jeffs, Rulon B. Jeffs, Samuel Jeffs, Seth Jeffs, William Jeffs, Benjamin Jessop, Jacob Harker, Mormon Jessop, Parley Harker, Terrill Harker, Wendell Jessop, Robert Jessop, Ben Nielsen, Merril Nielsen, Wendell Nielsen, Ben Rohbock, Jameson Rohbock, and Rulon Rohbock.

As I watched the boys climb off the bus, I began to feel the weight of responsibility that I, as the oldest, and all the older boys would be expected to shoulder by our parents and people. That night, in prayer, I pled with God to place in me the love and care of a parent for these boys.

As soon as the boys were all unloaded, I had them gather at the entrance of Hamilton House and read to them who they would be checking in with, which house and room they would be living in, and the rules and boundaries we had. After this, we hauled all their luggage to their respective rooms while they explored the place.

Each of the boys brought several toys with them and almost every bag had one or two remote control cars in it. CPS and several of the volunteer groups had purchased many toys for the children in San Angelo. After the boys brought their bags to their rooms, they ran up to the fishing ponds. In 2005, Father had taught us at the YFZ ranch that having toys was idolatrous and sinful, causing selfishness. Children were supposed to learn how to work and use tools. Playing games and having toys had been outlawed. Because of this, we felt it our duty to get rid of the toys. Several of us older boys gathered many of the toys up and threw them away. The boys were so busy fishing that they hardly realized the toys were gone. When they did, we reminded them what we were taught, and they made sure any remaining toys were destroyed.

We now had 54 boys at Cal Farley's Boys Ranch. All the 27 who arrived from the Pavilion were between the ages of 5 and 11 years. The two youngest were Seth Jeffs (my brother) and Terrill Harker, both the age of 5 years. We were not allowed any interaction with the other children at Boys Ranch. Notwithstanding the name "Boys Ranch," it is a facility for both boys and girls.

After a little while, we called the boys into prayer and reading. I told them the rules of the ranch and that we were going to carry out our religious rules to the best of our ability. I made a rule at that time (for which I was grateful ever after) of having all the boys 12 years and younger in bed by 8:00 pm.

As we were settling the boys in bed, they told us the story of the group of children being separated at the Pavilion earlier that day. They had gone a week being separated from their mothers and had watched out carefully for each other. In their anger, they became rude to all the staff and resisted everything CPS wanted them to do.

When the children realized their group was going to be broken up, they gathered in a large group with the older girls encircling all the younger children. They had a standoff that lasted several hours with hundreds of frightened children praying, crying, screaming, and begging CPS and law enforcement not to separate siblings from each other. After some time, with many threats of forceful separation, CPS was able to calm the group enough to promise the boys they would all be going to one place where many of their older brothers were. Although they disbelieved CPS, they finally separated and boarded the buses to come to Boys Ranch. The boys were traumatized by this experience, yet they found comfort in being allowed to come live with us.

Nearly all of us had siblings scattered around the state in different facilities hundreds of miles apart. Of my mother's children, her two younger boys, Jacob and Joseph, were with me. My sister Josephine was at High Sky Children's Ranch near Midland, and Amber was in a Baptist Children's shelter in Gonzales. All these places were hundreds of miles apart. We were not allowed any form of contact with each other.

We rearranged where everyone lived, and seven of my younger brothers moved in with me. They were: Seth (5yrs), William (6yrs), Samuel (6yrs), Kendall (7yrs), Joseph (8yrs), Nephi (9yrs), and Jacob (10yrs). It proved to be quite a chore to put the boys to bed at night. We older boys suddenly had placed upon us a mom and dad's responsibility, and this was a new experience. In addition, these children had now suffered a lot of emotional damage. All they wanted was to be with their mom and dad.

At midnight, when I was finally preparing for bed, Joseph came tumbling off his top bunk onto the floor and started crying. I picked him up and placed him on my bed. I slept nearby on the floor that night. In the morning, my mattress was wet, so I traded him mattresses.

Day 21

When morning came, I discovered that four of the boys in my room had a bed wetting trouble. They had been overcoming it at home, but since the raid started, they had regressed. To add to the problem, they only had a few pairs of clothes, and the washers were constantly running. I had considerable trouble keeping sufficient towels stocked up for them. I can still hear Joseph's shivering voice wailing in the bathroom, "Aaaammon, I need a towwellll!" I helped the boys get up and start in the shower. We only had three bathrooms in the house, so they were always crowded in the mornings and evenings. Taking care of so many children was overwhelming, but I put my head down and did my duty. I had chosen to stay for this very reason and didn't feel like there was any other recourse. I saw the boys regressing into childhood frailties they had been outgrowing. I felt their pain and insecurity. I could not fill the void their parents left but knew I must do my best.

First thing in the mornings after everyone was dressed, we went to the living room and had morning prayers. By the time prayer time was over, the staff had our breakfast ready, which usually consisted of bacon, sausage, eggs, and potatoes.

Brandon Steed was just 2 days younger than me. He turned 18 on April 23. CPS and Boys Ranch asked him to sign papers like I did. Brandon was the oldest boy living in Tunnel Home. He was mature and responsible. Brandon was essential to the success we had tending all the younger boys at Boys Ranch. He was very kindhearted, and all the boys loved him.

That day, the first group of us who had come to Boys Ranch had our DNA and fingerprints taken. We didn't want it, but Judge Walther had ordered our DNA be taken so CPS could verify that our parents were who we claimed they were. The people who took our cheek swabs were very courteous to us.

Chapter Thirteen

Teenagers Tending Kids

U s older boys felt overwhelmed at first in handling the day-to-day responsibilities of taking care of the young boys. We were used to hard manual labor, but we had never taken the responsibility of tending a large group of younger children. We were happy that CPS allowed so many of us to be in one location, but we had never been so grateful for our parents as we were now. Tending kids was a big job.

Boys Ranch staff bought many fishing poles and a mountain of tackle for us. All the boys were excited about fishing and spent all day at the two fishing ponds. I spent my time rigging the fishing poles and casting lines out for the boys. By the end of the day, I was exhausted.

That night at midnight, just as I sat down on my bed, my little brother Seth fell off his bunk onto the floor right at my feet. He started crying, so I picked him up, comforted him, and put him to sleep on my bed. As soon as he was settled, Joseph came rolling off his top bunk, just like he had the previous night. He hit his head on the nightstand on his way to the floor, and I was afraid he was badly hurt. I ran over and picked him up. As I carried him out into the hall, Jim Taylor, a Boys Ranch staff, came running into my room, wondering what all the noise was. We examined Joseph. He was unhurt, so we took him back into the room. We placed his mattress on the floor and settled him on it. Then Leslie Steed and I picked up Kendall on his mattress and placed it on the floor, also. Jacob had the other top bunk in the corner of the room, but he was a still sleeper, so I left him up there. After this, the boys in my room who had a top bunk slept on the floor until Boys Ranch provided railings for the beds.

Day 22

The next day, we spent most of our time at the fishing ponds. The staff promised the boys they would make sure each one had their personal tackle and tackle box. That day, one of the financial managers of Boys Ranch brought a carload of toys and more fishing poles. The staff asked us what we wanted to do with them. We told them we would take the toys and oversee the distribution because we were afraid to tell them that toys were no longer allowed in our culture. We didn't want them to use our removal of the toys against us. We felt intense pressure to live strictly by every rule we had been given at home. We thought if we did not, Father wouldn't allow us to return there. We considered it a special privilege to live in "Zion."

Day 23

On the 25th of April, Terry Cooper, manager of the staff in both homes we were staying in, brought me a paper with the names of more boys who were coming from the Coliseum in San Angelo. I decided which older boy would oversee each of them and discussed our responsibilities with each of the older boys. I also made a list of who would be in each house and each bedroom.

About noon, Terry Cooper called me aside and told me that although the boys who came up from the Pavilion had ended up accepting and having confidence in us, he was sure the boys coming from the Coliseum would not. He told me that the Boys Ranch staff who were volunteering in San Angelo had called him and told him of the terrible experience the mothers and children had gone through the day before at the Coliseum. He explained the trauma the separation had been on the staff alone. He was sure these boys would be more devastated than those who had come from the Pavilion, and therefore would not have any confidence in us older boys. After he finished speaking to me, I told him I knew these boys, and I was sure they would have confidence in us. He seemed surprised at my reply but said, "I guess we'll see."

At 3:55 pm, the boys from the Coliseum arrived. They appeared to be shaken up, but better behaved than those who had come from the Pavilion three days previous. Unlike the boys from the Pavilion, these boys had been with their mothers until the 24th. The influence of children being with their mothers, even after living through the rigid conditions CPS imposed in the Coliseum was quite notable to me. Another difference I noted was their open hostility toward CPS. They were livid about the trauma CPS had just put them through.

They told us about their separation from their mothers. They watched their younger siblings be torn from their mother's arms, screaming and crying. Then they gathered their siblings and tried to comfort and care for them. Shortly afterward, CPS also tore their younger siblings from them and separated them onto different buses, sending them to shelters hundreds of miles distant. These boys felt like they were failing their younger siblings by not fighting harder to be kept together. It was a sad time. I sought to comfort these young boys and let them know they had done their best. The sadness and concern we all felt for our siblings we were separated from was constantly with us.

We asked Terry Cooper if we could call Randy Shell, the CPS worker who brought us to Boys Ranch. He allowed it, and we talked to him for a while, begging him to do all he could to help us and our siblings get back together. We were angry at how scattered we were from each other, and Johnny threatened him that if he didn't do this, we were going to escape and find our siblings ourselves. He pled with us to not do anything rash and promised he would do all he could to help us out.

The boys who arrived from the San Angelo Coliseum were: Quincy Jeffs, Rawland Barlow, David J. Jeffs, Rulon Keate, Eli Barlow, Matthew Barlow, Abram Jessop, William Johnson, David Jeffs, Ammon W. Jeffs, Jeremiah Jeffs, Paul Jeffs, David Jessop, Richard Samuel Jessop, Daniel Lindsay, Raymond Jessop, Brett Barlow, and Richard Jeffs.

We now had 72 boys at Cal Farley's Boys Ranch, 36 in each house. Sixteen of the boys were my brothers.

All 72 Boys at Cal Farley's Boys Ranch

One day, Luke Benton, Mike Whitecotton, and some more of the staff brought four canoes and wanted us to go canoeing on the ponds with them. Several of the boys did so for a while that afternoon. Most of us older boys did not; in 2003, Father had started teaching us that it was wrong and dangerous to go out on any body of water in a boat. He said the devil had control of the waters. I had the boys who were checking in with me stay out of them. While the boys were canoeing around, one of them tipped over with one of the boys under it. Brandon Steed jumped in and rescued him. Of course, this confirmed to us how dangerous the waters were. That night, we heard Mr. Cooper, the staff manager, giving a report to CPS and heard him tell them that he noticed none of the older boys would go out on the water. At first, we were wary of him and did not know whether we could trust him, but soon learned he was there as our friend.

At first, we only had men for our staff, but after a week, it was both men and women. We were guarded in our behavior towards the female staff as we had been taught to be. I suppose we appeared rude to them, although it was a result of our raising and was unintentional. They didn't like it and told us we needed to look at them and smile at them, exactly what we had been taught not to do. Father always told the boys and girls to treat each other like snakes. We were told to have no interaction with other females outside of our families without his approval. This made the boys ignore them more.

I asked the staff if I could get a camera and a voice recorder. They seemed concerned and said they would see. Terry Cooper talked to me later and told me they were concerned that we would use these instruments to bring evidence against them. I assured him they were only for personal use and records, so he agreed to get them. Mark Strother ended up getting me the equipment.

One night, Terry Cooper asked me to come talk to him out in his car where we could have a private conversation away from the staff and other boys. I had already put the boys to bed, and it was late. I got in his car with him. He told me he was very concerned about the pressure I was taking and was worried that the responsibility and stress was going to cause me a nervous breakdown. After listening to him for a while, I said, "I rely on God for strength. I know He can help me. He will deliver us and make a way for us to go home." It was comforting to know he was looking out for me, and I could discuss how I felt without fear. He asked me about the toys he had noticed were disappearing. I told him we threw them away because they made the children fight and be selfish. He said he could understand our take on that and asked that we return the rest of the toys instead of throwing more away. This I agreed to. We also decided to spread the responsibility to the seven oldest as a committee, so I wouldn't be overstressed.

Terry Cooper told me the shortest time we would be in custody would be six months and a year was more likely. I had also been informed of this by several of our attorneys. When he told me this, I responded that we didn't feel like we could survive in custody for more than two months. I did not think it would be longer than that. He was surprised but told me he hoped it would be so. A day or two later, one of the boys who had kept their iPod let him listen to a song that had been composed and recorded at home called, "Cry Night and Day for Deliverance." That night, he told me that after he listened to that song, he could understand why we had so much faith in being delivered.

Soon after the boys from the Coliseum came, Julie Thompson, an employee of Boys Ranch, came to be one of our main staff. Within the first twenty minutes of her being there, we found there was going to be plenty of friction and drama with her. She walked into the kitchen where the boys were cleaning up dinner. One of the boys had thrown some food away, and she tried cornering him and making him eat it. He slipped away from her and ran off. Joshua Nielsen was right there and said something rude to her. She came towards him and swung her foot at him, playing like she was kicking him. He said, "Wow, you remind me of the devil!" She gasped and said, "That's the first time I've ever been called that." My brother Matthew was at the sink, and he told her, "If you take one step closer to me, I'm going to squirt you." She stepped closer, and he squirted her in the face. She told him to get her a rag to wipe off her face, so he ran to the dirty laundry and got her one. She started wiping off her face and then said, "Ugh, this towel stinks!"

That evening, Julie called for "the seven" to meet with her. I was busy putting my younger brothers to bed and did not want to talk to her. She demanded that I come. As soon as the boys were settled, I came. She handed me a schedule that called for each room leader to do a headcount on the boys who were in their room every two hours, all hours of the day and night. It was also scheduled in military time. I looked it over and told her we did not go by military time, nor did we stay up all night. This surprised her, as she had been led to believe we did. I asked her to revise it, and we would reconsider it. She took the papers back, and the subject was never brought up again. Later, they hung up a board with our pictures on it and had us pin our picture under a title that said which house we were in or if we were outside playing or fishing. This was the most successful way they kept track of everyone.

One day, we got a new staff worker named Ben Cunningham. We had been overwhelmed with the job of working with the younger boys, and the house had not been cleaned up to his satisfaction. He gathered us at 10 am and reprimanded us severely. He went too far and made us angry. I should not have minded, but I sent my friend Johnny to reprimand him back. He told Ben he was unreasonable for scolding us when we were busy tending the younger boys and needed to have some heart. Mr. Cooper was in the room with us when Mr. Cunningham scolded us, so he gathered us later and consoled our angry feelings. He told us he could see how difficult this was for us after all we were doing to have someone come scold us.

When the younger boys came to Boys Ranch, several volunteers from Cal Farley's organization who had been staff at the shelters in San Angelo came to Boys Ranch to be staff at our houses for a week. They felt an attachment to the boys after spending time with them in San Angelo. However, it created some difficulty as the younger boys considered anyone they remembered from shelters in San Angelo an enemy and treated them rudely. One of them was Mr. Davis, his wife, and two other ladies from a shelter called "Girlstown" in Lubbock. (Also part of the Cal Farley's organization) Mr. Davis was an ex-marine. He posted rules in military style. One of his rules I well remember posted on the west hall door of Tunnel Home: "You Shall Not use this door when entering or exiting the house." The boys were careful to disobey the rules he set up and there was a lot of friction with him.

One day, Terry Cooper asked the seven oldest of us boys to come talk with him. We sat on the west end of the big lawn south of Tunnel Home, watching the boys as we discussed the friction we had with several of the staff. While sitting there, we watched many of the boys run up the hill by Hamilton House. The staff had ordered us to keep off it, claiming there were rattlesnakes up there. As soon as Mr. Davis saw them, he went charging up after them. The boys saw him, and all went running down the other side, hollering, "Here comes the devil!" When Mr. Davis got to the top, there were no boys up there. As soon as he got back to the bottom of the hill, they all went tearing back to the top. We watched it all, and Mr. Cooper said, "There, that is what I am talking about!" I don't remember all the agreements we came to, but he said he would meet with staff and help them understand us better. We told him we would take care of the behavior problems with the boys. He said he would make sure the staff understood that. He told us he could see we were different from the other non-FLDS boys at Boys Ranch and had come to the maturity level they were working with the other youth on the campus to come to. He would make sure the staff understood that they were secondary to us older boys regarding working with the younger boys. After this, everything moved along a lot smoother.

Another time, when Terry Cooper was talking to me, he said, "Either you boys are professionals at putting on a show 24 hours a day, or else many allegations against your people are not true. I have been watching you with the younger boys secretly to see if you are abusive to the younger boys, and I have never seen you do anything that abusers are known to do." He expressed his belief that we had been lied about and knew we weren't putting on a show. He told me he could see that we were required to live a higher moral life than mainstream society in America did.

Chapter Fourteen

Surviving

Day 24

We were told that a CASA worker would be visiting us. We cleaned the house well and were all ready. CASA had seemed nice when we first met them at Fort Concho, but we had learned they recommended to Judge Barbara Walther that we remain in state custody, contrary to our wishes.

On Sunday morning, Connie Gauwain, a CASA worker, came. We met her outside of Hamilton house. All the boys gathered around her in a circle and started asking questions. They all asked her why she told the judge that we needed to stay in custody. She tried explaining that it was because they did not feel like it was in our best interest. She gave no other reasons. This only created an uproar among the younger boys. They clearly let her know she was wrong, telling her she had lied to the judge. Everyone was shouting at her that she told them one by one that she would tell the judge exactly what they wanted. All they had told her was they wanted to go home. The uproar made her uncomfortable and uneasy. We finally calmed the boys, and Joshua Nielsen showed her through the house so she could see we were being well cared for. We felt she was not our friend and was working against our interests.

Life began to take on a degree of normalcy; at least, it started to feel that way. Thankfully, humans can adapt to their circumstances, even in great difficulty. We learned to survive and have fun while doing so. There was always plenty of banter and light-hearted teasing between the boys. And plenty of wrestling. There were no moms to stop us from doing this anymore.

Mark Strother gathered us older boys and told us he would be flying to a meeting in Austin that CPS had called. They wanted to help everyone in the different shelters understand how to work with us better. He asked us if there was anything we wanted him to say if he had an opportunity to speak. We had two requests: we wanted to go home, and we wanted siblings to be reunited.

While Mark was gone, I learned from some of the mothers who I called on my cell phone that there were going to be dissidents from our people at that meeting. We became suspicious that this was a ruse by CPS to prejudice the staff against us. When Mark returned, we felt like his demeanor towards us was different and he was not as kind and outgoing as he had formerly been. We asked him who else was there at the meeting. He gave us the names of Brent Jeffs and Carolyn Jessop. We had been told they were terrible apostates from our church, so we treated him coldly and were careful around him.

The next day, Mark gathered all the room leaders and asked us to please not withdraw our confidence from him. He endeavored to explain to us that the people at the meeting didn't really say anything negative about us. He didn't believe everything they had said but would have to see if it was all true. He also told us we needed to not harass the female staff. He said we were harassing them by not paying them attention, and they were going home crying every night. I told him that we had been taught to be respectful but separate from females. This satisfied him and was not brought up anymore.

The next day, because I was busy taking care of the young boys, I asked Merril and Johnny to go speak with Mark again and see what he honestly thought about us now. They got an appointment with him in his office at headquarters. Dan Adams, the CEO of Cal Farley's was there also. They talked with Mark for quite a while.

Johnny told Mark "Ammon doesn't trust you anymore." This was because he had listened to the dissidents from our people. We thought they were the most wicked people on earth. This appeared to greatly affect Mark.

After they finished speaking, Dan Adams told them he knew Mark to be an honest man and trusted him completely. Dan and Mark talked with Johnny and Merril for a long time, working out all their prejudices. The boys left the office on much better terms with Mark and agreed in leaving that we would share the hot dog roast the entire ranch were having that evening when they did their ball game. After this, we all felt better towards Mark, who has always remained a true friend.

At this point, we were just surviving from day to day. We tried hard to keep the boys occupied and busy, though there was little to do besides playing games and fishing. We were used to an environment of hard manual labor where recreation had been ruled out.

Tim Job offered to take us on horse rides, which we were happy for. Most of the boys had never been on horseback. He took us on several trail rides out on the desert and through the hills. After the trail ride, he let us ride our horses around in the rodeo arena.

Soon after the younger boys came to Boys Ranch, they were sent to the clinic for checkups. I went with a group of boys that included most of my brothers. They were going through their check-ups fine until it came to my brother Samuel. Tommy Brian, the RN, saw Samuel and didn't know he had a prosthetic leg. He called me into his office alone and asked me what was wrong with Samuel's leg. "Are those broken bones sticking out?" he asked apprehensively. I told him that Samuel was born without a leg, and it was the awkward angle of his prosthetic leg he could see. As soon as he heard this, a look of great relief came over his face. When

Samuel had his check-up, I told Tommy Brian that he needed to get a new leg. After he examined it, he decided the same, so they set up an appointment in Amarillo for Samuel to get a new prosthesis.

A few days later, staff took Samuel to Amarillo for a checkup. Mitchel Jeffs and Ammon Steed went along with him. They met the doctor, explained our situation, and told him about the raid. The doctor kindly agreed that he would do the leg free of charge.

One day, we were all fishing in the ponds. The boys became tired of fishing and found an old log, which they rolled into the pond. The boys challenged each other to get on the log and float across the pond. Levi Steed volunteered and we all watched while he climbed on. It promptly rolled over, dumped him into the water, and floated off. Some of the boys cast their fishing lines out at the log, trying to catch it and bring it back, so we could try again. Staff noticed the commotion and came to see what we were up to. When they saw Levi Steed soaking wet and the log floating in the water, they told us we must not try riding on the log again. Josh Nielsen replied, "Okay. We won't get back on the log until the log floats back!" Everyone burst out laughing while staff assured us it was too dangerous to try again.

Day 33

On May 5, two CPS caseworkers, Daniel Medrano and Allison Fowler, visited us and finally allowed us to call our parents. Helaman, Abraham, Jacob, Joseph, William, and I got to talk to Mother Annette for about twenty minutes for the first time since April 14th. When I returned to the living room, to my surprise, one of the younger boys was holding one of Allison Fowler's earrings. Another boy was helping her take out the other one. She was crying. I talked to her and found the boys had told her all about their hatred for CPS and the injustices CPS had done to us. She had not been a part of the raid and was unaware of all that had happened. She told me she was considering quitting her job as a CPS worker after finding this out. Meanwhile, the boys had been telling her that earrings were evil, and she should remove them, which she did to appease them.

Daniel Medrano brought a list detailing the shelters all the children from the YFZ ranch had been taken to. We asked him if we could see the list. He agreed. Mahonri took pictures of each paper before we returned them. This is how we learned where all our siblings were located.

We began efforts to find ways of escape and an underground route to our parents. One day the staff forgot to lock the office where the house alarm system was. We saw this as our chance to bypass them. While we worked on the window alarm, one boy would stand in the office and turn off the alarm whenever it started to beep. We opened my bedroom window and finally got the alarm to stop registering that it was open. For the rest of our stay there, my window stayed partially open. I used a sleeping bag to cover the opening. We also found a Boys Ranch security plan sheet in case something happened that would "jeopardize our safety." It was very helpful information as we made our underground plans. We kept our plans secretive. Only a few of the oldest boys there knew anything was afoot.

Mr. Cooper told us CPS was going to require us to get immunizations. All my life, we had been taught by our religious leaders that it was wrong to take any vaccinations. I informed Mr. Cooper it was against our religious beliefs to take vaccinations. He cautioned us against resisting, lest something terrible happen and we be separated and scattered. He took a few of us down to Mark's office to show us a paper detailing what the immunizations would be. Those of us who were older would have to be given over twenty different immunizations to bring us up to the CDC (Center for Disease Control) guidelines.

That night, after the boys had gone to bed, we older boys discussed the vaccines for several hours. We decided we would resist the immunizations being given because we did not trust anything the state wanted us to do. We were terribly worried the vaccines would contain dangerous toxins and even cause possible sterilization. We felt like the state had nefarious purposes in requiring this. We determined that if they were going to force us, we would block ourselves into one of the rooms in the Hamilton House with enough food and water for three days and fight our hardest against it. After this, we carefully hid any packaged food we could obtain under our beds in preparation for this scenario. We informed our parents, who also protested strongly against this until CPS backed down on the issue.

Day 34

On May 6, Luke Benton and some other Boys Ranch staff gathered up several bikes for the boys to ride. All day, the boys took turns riding the bikes around the field by our house. Bikes had been outlawed at the YFZ ranch and were new to many of the boys. The bikes quickly became a cause of much contention among the boys, and all day, I had to take care of their quarrels. The next day, Merril Jeffs and I went straight to the fishing ponds with the boys I was overseeing to avoid all the quarrels about the bikes that were certain to happen. I was perfectly willing for the other older boys to help resolve them. Within an hour or two, the younger boys started coming to me with their grievances against each other about the bikes. The day ended up being a repeat of the day before.

By late afternoon, many of the boys began manifesting a great deal of discontent for the situation we were in, and we had a lot of behavioral issues to deal with. In one instance, a lady who was in her late forties from Girlstown told my brother Jacob and Isaac, along with several of the other boys, to stop going over the fence and into the forested gulch by the west pond. It was out of bounds. They verbally took their frustration out on her. Jacob told her he was going to shoot her with an M16 rifle. Isaac told her they had secret plans to harm her. This made the staff very upset with us. This lady's coworker was so angry that she went into the staff quarters and declared she would not come out until it was time for them to return to Girlstown.

That night at our prayer time, Terry Cooper talked to all the boys about the problems that were between us and the staff. I asked Mr. Cooper to simply remove the bikes, as it was causing a great deal of fighting, and that it would be best to not have them for a time. All the boys agreed to this. Luke Benton gathered up the bikes the next day and took them. We put our efforts into other games and activities where all who wanted could participate.

After prayer time, I inquired among the boys and found out what had happened at the gulch. Once the younger boys were put to bed, we older boys gathered around the lady who had been threatened and told her we were very sorry. We explained that we had never known what an M16 rifle was until the cops brought them during the raid. We engaged in a lengthy conversation with her about the values we were raised with, and by the end, she was crying, expressing that we were the best boys she had ever met. She went and spoke to her offended coworker, convincing her to come back out of the staff quarters and associate with us again.

Every night, just before coming in for prayer and reading, we began playing games with the boys to wear them out so they would be tired at bedtime. We taught them games we had played when we were younger in the Salt Lake area and Short Creek. All games had been outlawed at the YFZ ranch.

During the first week of May, the homeschool packets (which were organized by people who were still on the YFZ ranch) for the boys were brought to Boys Ranch by Rulon Barlow, an FLDS trucker. After examination by the staff, they were given to us. We attempted to do school in the mornings with the boys. It was a haphazard school effort, but somehow, we managed to get a little done. I also conducted kindergarten with William, Samuel, and Seth. Although a full-time high school schedule was sent to us older boys, we were too busy with the younger boys to complete any of it. My younger brother Helaman often assisted me with the boys I was caretaker of, considering the significant task I had overseeing all the boys. I was also constantly diffusing the friction the boys had with the staff.

One Sunday morning after holding Sunday School, Leslie Steed and I took several younger boys for a walk around the ponds. Opting to go up the gulch, we climbed the fence and walked away from Boys Ranch for nearly an hour, covering about two miles. We reveled in our momentary freedom and wished we could just fly away and never return. We eventually decided to return before the staff discovered we were missing.

I had the ongoing responsibility of keeping up with the laundry for the boys in my room. One night, as I was taking my boys' laundry to wash, Joshua Nielsen was making fun of me because of how it reeked. I made no reply initially, but I eventually picked up a pair of wet long underwear and flung it at him. It hit him and wrapped around his head twice. He hastily tore it off in utter disgust and headed straight for the shower while the rest of us looked on and laughed heartily. It was good karma.

After my brother William had been there for two weeks, I realized he hadn't yet showered. I had been busy trying to keep up with the boys who had to shower daily because of their bed-wetting trouble, so I hadn't noticed. I told him that night to have a shower. He begged me to let him skip it, and I refused. He told me he had peed at night, but it had dried. When I learned this, I told him I would have to scrub him myself if he didn't take a shower immediately, so he finally complied. We developed a habit of smelling the boys' hair as soon as they came out of the shower to make sure they had used soap.

When my brother Samuel first came, I had to help him in the shower, but soon taught him how to shower by himself. He also learned how to take his prosthetic leg off and put it back on by himself. After a few weeks, he got his new prosthetic leg, which was much better than his old one. As soon as I learned how to take care of him, I made sure he took his prosthetic leg off each night before going to bed.

The younger boys had brought pajamas and I ensured they wore them at night. During the weeks at the shelters in Eldorado and San Angelo, the boys had slept in their day clothes. It seemed they felt more secure that way. I told them it was much easier to remove the smell from wet pajamas than it was from wet pants and shirts.

I had a hard time getting Seth, age 5, to bed at night. I finally found a remedy that I used when his energies were high. During prayer time, I would have him sit by me, put my arm around him, and hold him while I read. By the time I finished, he would be fast asleep in my arms. He just needed that comfort. After all the boys left the room, I would carry him to bed.

Seth was a funny boy. When he first came, he had no shoes, so we carried him around on our shoulders. Whenever we walked by a staff member who had a beard, he would tug on it. At night, when I helped him say his prayers, he would say, "In the name Jeez' Chris' amen!" as quickly as possible after each phrase because he wanted to hurry and be done. He was my youngest brother there.

Chapter Fifteen

"Take Away the T!"

"**G**uess what we saw today on our way back from Amarillo," Mitchel said.

"What was it?" we asked.

"There was a billboard with an advertisement for a Ford Escape. It said,

'Plant and Escape.'"

"Plant an Escape?"

"Yeah. Now let's take away the *T!* Let's *Plan* an Escape!"

We all chimed in excitedly. We were all in agreement. This was our challenge to solve. The older boys were unanimous in finding a way we could leave the ranch secretly. Sam and I were selected to begin scouting around and seeing if we could establish an underground communication with our parents. We began holding secret meetings where we discussed our plans and strategies in frustrating CPS' plans. To prevent leaking anything that absolutely could not make it to the staff without endangering ourselves, we only allowed those into the meetings who knew the countersign to the password "take away the t."

One morning when many of the young boys were fishing, Sam Jessop and I went to the back of the pond and climbed through the fence when no one was watching. There was a large gulch located on the west side of the large fishing pond full of willows and cottonwood trees. We crawled over to the gulch and down the bank. Then we walked across it and up into the desert brush, looking for the best route to the highway. It was hard to tell which route to take as we were unfamiliar with the countryside, but we were determined to find a way. We scouted around, seeking to find landmarks we could use at night in our escape attempts. There was a radio tower we believed was close to the highway and we decided that would be our destination next time. Knowing the staff was monitoring all of us, we made our venture quickly and then silently hiked back over to the ponds where we were supposed to be fishing.

That night, we were ready to make a real attempt. It was time to *"take away the t!"* The night was cold, so we donned black denim jackets and filled our pockets with granola bars. A few of the other boys helped us prepare. We silently climbed out of my window while they held the blinds still. Another stood at the bedroom entrance to make sure staff didn't discover our actions. We started off at 11:30 pm. We had to sneak across the lawn by the house, cross the street, and sneak across another large lawn until we got to a tree line by the bank of the ponds. We did this in total silence and were undetected by the staff or security officers. We were frighteningly exposed by the house and streetlights, but crawled on our hands and knees until we were out of the light. Immediately, a dog began barking at us, and we froze in our tracks, our hearts pounding fiercely. After it quieted down, we continued to the back of the ponds and climbed through the barbed-wired fence. We walked a few yards and were in the underbrush-filled gulch.

The cottonwoods grew thick down in the bottoms. The night was cloudy, windy, and very dark. I brought one flashlight but did not dare use it at first. We blundered our way along in the dark and stumbled down the banks into the underbrush until we could go no farther in the darkness. I pulled out my flashlight, and with my hand over the light, it emitted just enough for us to see. We began to make our way. We were still entirely unfamiliar with the area, although we had studied some aerial photos of the ranch that we had seen down at the ranch headquarters. Everything seemed much different at night than we had seen in the daylight. Just after emerging from the underbrush, we stumbled right into a swamp, with the mud going over and into our shoes, soaking our feet. Then, through willows and up the bank of the other side, we went, climbing through another fence. Now, we could see the flashing lights of the radio tower and set our sights on it.

Pressing forward, we stumbled into thick bushes six to seven feet tall. Not knowing any way around them, we pressed straight on through. It seemed these rough bushes would never end. We crossed a dirt road, which we didn't dare stay on, and pressed on towards the radio tower. After three-quarters of a mile, we came out of the bushes, feeling battered. To our dismay, we discovered the hillsides were covered in yucca, which poked us like needles until our knees were numb. It was so dark that I walked right into a barbed wire fence, which threw me onto my back. Then I started watching too closely and jumped at every stick I saw.

We finally made it to the radio tower at 12:30 am. We ate our granola bars and made a few phone calls. To finalize our adventure, we jumped another fence and ran across the highway and back, just in time to drop onto the ground as some vehicles came driving by. We felt flushed with success in accomplishing this much of our night's mission. While up there, my sisters Teresa and Josephine called from High Sky Children's Ranch on a secret phone Mother Annette had snuck to them at a visit. I was very happy to hear them and told them what I was up to. More cars were coming, so I started to run and slammed into another fence, which threw me to the ground again and tore my pants open. Sam, who was behind me, got a good kick out of me being a fence hitter, while my sisters who were on the phone wondered what all the commotion was.

We made our way back through the bushes. Sam was so thirsty that he nearly drank out of a filthy old cattle trough, but I convinced him to wait until we got back. Next was the wash, and along the ponds, we went until we were back in the light. We crept slowly across the lawns, hearts pounding, and made it to my window. We climbed in at 2:00 am and went to bed. Early the next morning, each of the older boys who had helped us sneak out came to see if we had made it back. I'm not sure whether they or we were under more stress. After this, we studied the aerial photos of the ranch much closer and noticed the dirt road we had crossed went directly to the highway, about halfway between the radio tower and the main entrance to the ranch. We thought it might be safe to walk up the road, but after some deliberation, we decided against it, as our tracks would be easy to find on the sandy road.

A couple of days later, we decided to try again and meet a few of Sam's brothers who would be passing through the area that night. We left the house at 11 pm. It took about an hour for us to make the 1.6 miles to the radio tower. At 12:30 am, Leroy Jessop, Raymond Jessop, and Jackson Jessop pulled off the road by the tower in a truck and stopped. Sam and I ran across the highway and jumped in with them. We were elated to finally meet some of our friends without being monitored. That feeling of a few moments of freedom is something I'll never forget! I'd never have gone back if it weren't for all the other boys who were still trapped at the ranch.

We had had a tornado drill earlier that day at our houses. A tornado watch had been issued that night. As it became stormy, we decided it was best to return to Boys Ranch before anything happened. The wind picked up, prompting us to ask for a drop-off at the dirt road. We ran all the way down it until we reached the gulch, then traversed through it back to the ponds and eventually back to the house.

A few days later, Sam, Mitchel, and I ventured out again. We walked through the bushes until we reached the radio tower. This time, Wally and Louis Jessop picked us up for a drive. We hoped to go into Amarillo, but they weren't comfortable taking us there yet. When they dropped us off, Louis and Wally walked all the way down to the ponds with us.

One day, I received a phone call while I was outside, so I rushed into one of the bedroom closets at Tunnel Home to answer it. It was my sister Rachel, and I was very glad to hear from her. As she was talking to me, one of the boys came running into the room and tried to open the door to the closet I was in. I tried holding it shut, but he gave a tremendous tug, and the door burst open. It was my brother, Jacob, staring in disbelief to see me with a cell phone, as he didn't know I had one. I had him solemnly promise not to tell anyone. Thankfully he kept his promise.

We spent a lot of time during the day on the field, running around with the boys or up at the ponds, fishing. Many of the boys became avid fishermen. When they became bored, they would float empty tackleboxes or water jugs on the ponds, reeling them in with their fishing poles. One day, a few boys caught some fish and ran a string through their mouth and gills, tying it to a water bottle. Then they'd release the fish. They could watch it swim all over the ponds. When we discovered what they were doing, we had them stop. We told them it was "fish abuse."

We originally had meals brought to both houses, but we arranged with staff to let us all eat at Hamilton House. This made meal clean up simpler. Since we had arrived, each room of boys would take a day to prepare for the food to be brought by setting up the tables, chairs, and setting the tables with dishes. After the meal, we did the kitchen cleanup.

On my kitchen day, as soon as the dishes were gathered, my boys would disappear, and several times, I spent hours washing dishes and cleaning up. However, I enjoyed it as it became my break time from tending to the boys.

The boys who were with me most of the time were my brothers Nephi, Joseph, Kendall, Seth, and cousins Quincy and David Jeffs. I also often kept my brother Rulon with me and made oatmeal mush for him when we had meals that he was intolerant to, because of his food allergies. My brother William was with me or Helaman each day.

On Friday, May 2nd, we decided to sneak out again. Sam, Johnny, Mitchel, and I went. We opted to use the dirt road this time, thinking it would be safe. When we reached the top of the road, we discovered a State Trooper about half a mile up by the hill the radio tower was on. He was watching for speeding cars. Terrified of being caught, we hid on the ground behind a small brush-covered dirt pile.

Sam called Wally Jessop, his brother, and told him that when he arrived, he needed to pull off on the east side of the road and leave his lights on. He misunderstood, and when he pulled up a few minutes later, he made a U-turn, parked on the west side of the road, and turned his lights off in full view of the officer.

With about 100 yards to run, we decided to go for it. We jumped up, ran up the dirt road, climbed the gate, crossed the cattle guard, ran across the highway, and jumped into his vehicle. The last two boys had oncoming car lights shining on them as they jumped in. As Johnny jumped in, we started off. The trooper noticed some commotion and followed us for several miles as we sat breathless and scared to death in the vehicle. We got to Amarillo and went to a house some of the mothers had rented and spent some time there. We gave them the pictures we had taken while at the ranch. It was most helpful to sit at the table and discuss how to take care of the boys with their parents. Around 2 am, Mormon Barlow took us back.

A week later, Merril Jeffs and Steven Dockstader accompanied me out. We were getting braver and decided to leave at 7 pm while it was still light. We were almost to the dirt road when someone in a suburban pulled up, stopped, and rolled down their windows. We dropped against the bank of the gulch and quietly ran back until we were in some thick willows. We wondered if the staff had missed us and were looking for us. I called Brandon Steed on his secret phone, but he hadn't heard any commotion among the staff. I decided to see what they were doing, so I crawled on my stomach for about 150 yards until only a large oak tree separated me from their sight. It was a man apparently enjoying an evening smoke. We had to wait him out, so I crawled back to the other two boys, who had been scared even farther back by a snake in the bushes. Then another vehicle drove up and stopped, so I crawled over there again to see if we were being looked for, but we were not.

After some time, they drove off, and we went through the bushes and up by the radio tower to wait for our ride. We noticed the State Trooper was there again, so we went over the hill and sat under some bushes close to the highway. Our ride was delayed, and we ended up sitting there for two hours. At 11 pm, Alan and Christopher Dockstader picked us up. They saw the trooper and were afraid he would notice their vehicle if they turned around, so they drove us on a long detour. We arrived in Amarillo very late. That night, we bought another voice recorder and more phones. When that was accomplished, we went back. Alan and Christopher drove us down the dirt road and dropped us off at the wash. This saved us a long walk back in.

Day 39

On the evening of May 11, the younger boys decided they wanted to wrestle us older boys down, so they did this for about an hour, and we had a good and exhausting time with them. When we came in, the staff asked us how we had stayed in one piece. Just before we went in, a crowd of younger boys was trying to get Mitchel down, and they finally succeeded, but in doing so, he fell on top of my brother Rulon. Right after our evening prayer time, Rulon started showing signs of a head injury, and kept vomiting severely. Mitchel and Richard watched him closely. We were very concerned, so the staff decided to run him to the hospital. He was there late into the night as the hospital monitored his vitals. He began recovering and they said he had a concussion.

Day 40

On May 12, I visited with my CPS caseworker, Sandra Hansen, along with Helaman, Richard, Rulon, Abraham, Jacob, Joseph, William, and a few of the other boys who were there. We were told parental visits would be starting soon. She asked us about our favorite hobbies and gave us all a low intensity interview. Some of the boys had such a bad image of CPS in their minds that they treated her very rudely. CPS informed us that they were our legal parents. We told them we would never respect that.

Day 42

On the morning of May 14, the first visits took place. One of the parents who came was Rich Jessop. CPS allowed his wife, Joy, who had brought clippers, to give many of the boys a haircut.

Terry Cooper, our staff manager, informed us that Carey Cockerell, the commissioner of the Texas Department of Family and Protective Services, would be coming to check on us. In preparation for his visit, we diligently cleaned the houses and surroundings. We wanted to impress him with our living conditions and make sure he could see no reason to split us up and send us to other shelters. That night, we allowed the younger boys to stay up, turning our house into a lively environment. I took the opportunity to write a letter to Mr. Cockerell, urging him to work towards reuniting us with our parents.

Day 43

On the morning of May 15th, Carey Cockerell arrived. He spent several hours in discussions with Dan Adams, the CEO of Boys Ranch, and Mark Strother, the ranch manager, at headquarters. Later in the morning, he toured the ranch. When he came up to the Tunnel Home to see us, he was accompanied by several assistants. Though he didn't say much, we showed him one of the bedrooms, and he seemed satisfied. I handed him the letter I had prepared. As I shook his hand, I asked, "Will you be sure to read it?" He assured me that he would. Notably, I later learned, this was two weeks after his testimony to the Senate Committee on Health and Human Services, where he stated that medical examinations had revealed numerous physical injuries to the children in State custody, justifying the Department's decision to retain custody. This was not true. There was not a higher percentage of children with injuries from the YFZ ranch than anywhere else in the country.

Weeks later, I learned that after visiting several shelters where children were held in state custody, Carey Cockerell declared that the boys at Cal Farley's Boys Ranch were in the best place and were the most well-situated. It's worth mentioning that we enjoyed the greatest freedom compared to other shelters, thanks to the trust the older boys had gained from the management during the initial week before the influx of younger boys. We also had been able to form "family units" and had some normalcy with routines we had brought from home.

Shortly after Mr. Cockerell's departure, Terry Cooper asked me to gather my brothers Joseph and Rulon. He informed me that they were supposed to go to Amarillo for an interview, clarifying that it would not be CPS conducting the interviews. The following day, Sam Jessop, Wendell Jessop, Ben Jessop, and David Jessop were also scheduled for interviews. Sam Jessop and I accompanied Rulon and Joseph to a small building called "The Bridge." After serving us a snack and letting the boys settle in, the investigators, dressed like our mothers to put us at ease, conducted interviews that lasted about an hour for each boy. I discreetly placed a voice recorder in Joseph's pocket before his interview.

Later that night, I listened to Joseph's interview on the voice recorder. Despite his nervousness, I could discern that he mentioned breaking his foot when he was little. They also subjected him to inappropriate sexual questions he couldn't comprehend. Joseph was only eight years old. Rulon, when asked about his interview, could only express uncertainty, stating, "I don't know; they just asked me so many questions."

The following day, as we headed to Amarillo in the morning, the investigators at The Bridge informed us that they didn't need to interview Sam anymore. We suspected this was because Sam was older and more defiant than they had expected. Sam insisted on being interviewed and confirmed our suspicions. This time, I discreetly placed the recorder in Wendell Jessop's shirt pocket behind a notebook. The boys went for their interviews two at a time, and the process took a considerable amount of time. Unable to contact the boys' attorneys, we waited anxiously. When it was over, Terry Cooper took us to lunch, and as we waited, Sam and I discussed the events. We realized that CPS had deceived us, presenting the interviews as conducted by unrelated individuals when, in fact, the recordings were handed over to CPS. Frustrated and feeling like CPS was on a witch hunt to justify our removal from home, I conveyed to Terry Cooper that we would not permit any more boys to be interviewed there. This decision greatly concerned him.

Upon our return to Boys Ranch, Mark Strother, the ranch manager, called the seven oldest boys down to his office at headquarters. Mark and Terry conveyed that if we were unwilling to let the boys go to Amarillo for questioning, we needed to have a "Plan B," or CPS might cause trouble, potentially leading to our separation. After pondering for a while, I suggested, "Tell CPS if they want to conduct interviews, they must send their own investigators here." Satisfied with this, they agreed to convey the message. That evening, during prayer time, I briefed the boys on the situation and asked if any of them wanted to go to Amarillo for an interview. Their resounding "NO!!!" echoed through the house. I followed up with, "Should we tell them to bring their own investigators here?" The unanimous "YES!!" reverberated throughout the house and beyond. I was grateful for the solidarity displayed by all the boys during this tense period, although I keenly felt the strain.

Day 44

On the afternoon of May 16, Terry Cooper informed me that CPS wanted a full-body X-ray done on Joseph. I protested and told him I wouldn't allow it unless he brought me the papers. I realized CPS was attempting to justify their statement on excessive broken bones being an issue at the YFZ ranch, although he had broken his foot when we lived in Short Creek. While he retrieved the papers, I went to my closet and called Mother Annette, informing her about it. Just as I came out, Terry entered the room with the papers and warned me that resistance could lead to more trouble. Seeing resistance would be useless, I asked four of the older boys to go accompany him. Samuel had an appointment, so he went as well. Mitchel accompanied Joseph into the X-ray room, where the nurse had him wear a lead vest. They made Joseph strip for the X-ray, but he refused to remove his long underwear. I called Mother Gloria and Mother Sharon, who were staying in Amarillo, and informed them that Samuel would be there for an appointment. They knew the location of the prosthetist and showed up while the boys were there, getting a chance to visit with them without CPS present.

Sam and I slipped off the ranch that evening and true to his Friday night custom, the state trooper was by the radio tower again. We brought the recordings from the interviews at The Bridge, a copy of my letter to Carey Cockerell, and the papers from CPS about the X-rays they required on some of the boys to see if their previous record of broken bones had been the result of abuse. We left at dusk and easily made our way to the tower. This time, our ride arrived promptly, and Lehi Allred pulled off right where we told him to. We jumped into the truck. He had Mothers Monica and Brenda with him. We went into Amarillo, dropped off the papers to the mothers, and visited with several of the parents there about their boys. We returned to Boys Ranch at 4 am.

Chapter Sixteen

Visits

We went a long time at Boys Ranch without parental visits. CPS took a month getting any schedule established for us. The boys continually queried when their parents were going to come visit them. This was hard. A few of us older boys had secret phones, but the younger boys could only communicate through monitored calls. And that rarely happened. A phone call could not make up for a visit. The boys became anxious to see their parents.

One morning, Terry Cooper brought his laptop and an overhead projector to Hamilton House to show all the boys the videos and slideshows the FLDS had made and presented to the public after the raid about how happy we had been at the ranch. Another slideshow showed the sadness the children were experiencing because of the raid. They were on a website owned by the church. All the boys gathered in the living room to watch. I was unable to hold back my tears while we watched, but I tried to be strong for the boys and hid my tears.

It weighed heavily upon me to see many of the boys becoming contentious and angry because of the trauma and being pent up in a situation so different from home. I felt constantly required to stand up to the staff to maintain our stringent religious requirements. It was a constant, unseen battle. I keenly felt the weight of the expectations of the parents upon me to keep their boys steadfast in the way they had raised them.

Day 45

Our first visit with Mother Annette was scheduled for May 17. We hadn't seen her for more than a month. We were very excited. Our caseworker allowed us a four-hour visit that day. We were overjoyed to finally see her. Mother Shannon also came and visited with Seth and Kendall. The last two hours of our visit, they let all of us be together. Mark took us around Boys Ranch, after which we walked down to the horses with our caseworker. I was feeling a lot of stress at the time and did not talk much at all. Mother Annette brought a binder with photos of my siblings during their visits with her. I spent a long time looking at that book. I was able to talk to Mother Shannon about working with Seth, as he was quite a handful.

When we finally had to go, William begged Mother Annette to take him with her. She had just given him a new blanket, which he had draped around his shoulders. She hugged him, and they both cried. It was hard to gather the boys up and walk back to our house while they left. On our way to the house, we all gave vent to our feelings in a flood of tears. We stood on the field south of Tunnel Home for a long time in silence. My brothers looked sad and forsaken as we watched the mothers drive off. The sky was mostly cloudy, and a gentle breeze stirred the warm, sultry air. The scent of fresh, green grass filled the air while white, fluffy seeds from the tall cottonwoods wafted to the ground. We could hear youthful laughter as the other boys played near the houses we lived in. It suddenly felt like we had been there forever. Home began to seem so distant. How long would this nightmare last?

On each visit day, Mark Strother would take our parents who came for visits on a tour around Boys Ranch in a bus. When he came by our houses, he refused to stop because CPS could get him in trouble for stopping. After our visit this day, we decided we would stand in a line across the road and make him stop. When he came, we were all waiting and stood our ground. This made him upset, and he told our parents that he wouldn't do any more tours if we blocked his way. When I met him late that afternoon, he still seemed angry. He asked me why we blocked him, threatening that he wasn't going to do tours for a week now. I told him we felt like we had to make him stop just once when CPS wasn't watching. I realized he was under a lot of pressure from state oversight in our case to do everything just right.

After visits began at Boys Ranch, there were visits almost daily throughout the week. The visits took place in a large building near the ranch headquarters, about a five-minute walk from the houses we stayed in. Our schedule became a constant round of taking boys to their parents' visits, attorney visits, CASA visits, and wellness checkups.

I was called to visit my CASA worker one day. Many of my brothers also had CASA workers visiting them at the same time. My CASA worker was responsible for three of us boys. He was kind and quietly told me that he felt like we ought to be returned to our parents. He requested me to keep what he said quiet, as he did not think that was what his organization wanted. I was very impressed with his demeanor towards us. While he was interviewing me, William, Samuel, and another boy were close by, talking to their CASA worker. I was watching and listening to them. The lady would ask William a question. Will, age 6, would say, "I'm not going to tell you if you're going to tell the judge!" She would explain to him that her job was to talk to him and then tell the judge what he had to say. Then she would ask her question again, and he would reply, "I'm not going to tell you if you're going to tell the judge!" She looked at me helplessly and I told Will he could tell her whatever he wanted to, but he refused to give any other reply. He had come up with that answer with no coaching and apparently felt like the judge was responsible for severely upending his life. He wanted nothing to do with her.

Chapter Seventeen

A Glimmer of Hope

"**I**s anything being done that will make so we can go home soon?" we wondered. Most of us knew our status hearings were taking place in San Angelo. The status hearing is where the judge and other parties to the case review the service plan CPS makes for the parents, but they generally are not considered an opportunity to re-litigate whether the child should have been placed in state custody. Our attorneys told us these hearings wouldn't change our situation. We hoped for a miracle.

Day 50

On May 22nd, Terry Cooper gathered us all into the living room at the Hamilton House. He told us the Third Court of Appeals had held an emergency hearing on a writ of mandamus some of the mothers' attorneys had filed. A writ of mandamus is a remedy that can be used to compel a lower court or inferior government official to properly fulfill their official duties or correct an abuse of discretion. When someone files a petition for a writ of mandamus, they must show that they have no other remedy available. It is different than an appeal. That certainly seemed to fit our case. The appellate court had determined that the state was wrong to consider the entire ranch one household and that any abuse claims could only apply to individual households. He told us they gave the 51st district court, where Judge Barbara Walther was district judge, ten days to vacate the order that had allowed them to take us into custody. We were surprised and overjoyed. We had no idea this hearing was even happening. While the writ of mandamus had been filed by a few of the mothers' attorneys, we hoped it would be applied to the cases of all the children who had been removed from the YFZ ranch. Mr. Cooper quickly dampened our joy by telling us CPS was not likely to send us home immediately. He suspected they would file an appeal. A few hours later, Mr. Cooper informed us that CPS would be appealing this decision to the Supreme Court of Texas, and he was unsure what the outcome would be. He gave us no encouragement about going home.

Late that night, Mr. Cooper talked to us older boys and said he had read the decision of the Third Court of Appeals and was confident the Supreme Court would uphold it. However, he didn't want us to raise our hopes too high. We held onto this glimmer of hope and felt extremely anxious about the outcome. All the court hearings before this had seemed hopeless and discouraging. CPS kept up a good front and continued forward in our cases like nothing was about to change.

Day 51

The next visit for Mother's and Mother Annette's boys was on Friday, the 23rd of May. Our caseworker was not there, so Kathy Brown and Rebecca Ames, both CPS workers, monitored our visit. They were stricter than our caseworker and refused to allow my brother Levi to come into our visit, so I gave them a lot of grief over it. CPS was given the discretion to decide whether to allow additional family members to visit us along with our mothers. After our visit, we waited by our house for a few hours for Mark to bring the parents around on their tour of the place. Dan Adams, CEO of Boys Ranch, happened to be there and gave the tour. When he came by our houses, he stopped the bus and opened the doors so the boys could see their mothers again. He won our hearts by this action and will be remembered as one who was always kind and proved our friend the whole way through.

Mr. Cooper informed us that CPS ordered them to take our iPods, cameras, and anything like that from us. We couldn't understand why. We felt like they were tyrannical. We returned the camera Mark purchased for us back to him, gathered up some of the iPods for staff to keep, hid more of them and a few phones in the bathroom walls and the attic. Sam, Johnny, and I had begun to seriously plan an escape from

Boys Ranch with all the boys. I know it sounds crazy now, but we were dead serious at the time. We had determined if the state courts refused to allow our release, we would find a different way out.

Brandon decided the best place to hide his phone would be down by headquarters in some old irrigation pipe. He put his phone in a plastic bag and pushed it partway up the pipe. Then he came and told me what he had done. I told him I didn't like the idea of having it away from us where we couldn't control what happened to it. He went down to get it back, and a squirrel had dragged it out of the pipe and pulled the phone out of the bag. This scared all of us because we knew our houses would be thoroughly searched if anyone caught wind of us having phones there.

We slipped out and went to Amarillo that evening and bought hats and other items to help us blend in better with the outside world. We were looking for camo clothes but couldn't find any that night. We also purchased a camera and picked up a laptop that one of the parents had provided for us. This time, we made it back at 3 am.

By now, I was tired of worrying about the lights on the house and streetlights when we would sneak out during the night. So, one afternoon, Sam and I went to work on them. Sam first disengaged a light on Tunnel Home while I climbed partway up a power pole and unscrewed the bulb of a streetlight. There was also a streetlight by the big pond. I couldn't climb up to it, so we stood under it and started throwing rocks at it. We were way too obvious, so we went back into the trees behind the bank of the pond and did our target practice at the light. After trying for a while, I finally hit the bulb. After the deed was done, we innocently walked out of the trees and into Tunnel Home.

Day 52

On May 24th, many of the boys had visits, so we did not do much throughout the day. As it was a holiday weekend, we had different staff than usual. They did not know us as well. That afternoon was hot, so I went to my room with the boys for a couple of hours to cool off and relax while the younger ones played with blocks and an electric train I had kept under my bed. I had chosen to keep it when staff had given us more toys and decided it was fine to have some toys because of our situation. Later, I asked one of the boys to bring us some milk so we could have a snack of cold cereal in my room. Robert Miller, who was the head of staff that day in our house, wouldn't let the boys bring any milk to my room, so I went and got it myself. Robert Miller was upset and told me he could go get Mark to come reprimand me if he needed to. I told him to go right ahead as I saw no problem with anything we were doing. By now, it was about 6 pm.

Ammon Steed and I went up on the hill and were talking everything over, telling each other stories about the first week of the raid. We got behind some bushes and were looking at some pictures I had taken on my phone during the first week of the raid that he had not seen. Our staff began acting strangely and spread all around the ponds and through the bushes, watching us closely. I realized that us staying in our room all afternoon, eating cereal, and then running up the hill had made the staff think we were planning on running away. I thought this hilarious, because we had been sneaking out right under their noses for weeks, and they had no idea about it. As soon as we realized what they were thinking, we jumped in and played along with it. As the rest of the older boys saw what was going on, they, too, joined us on the hilltop. Many of the younger boys added to the chaos and led the staff along in their false assumptions. It created a great sensation among them, and they called Terry Cooper, who was on vacation, to come save the day. We were having a great time until Terry Cooper came driving up. Then we realized they were dead sure we were about to be runaways. We seven oldest boys ran down to his car and he had us hop in with him. He took us for a drive off Boys Ranch and told us that staff had told him we had a plan in place and were trying to run away. We told him all about the staff becoming upset about eating food in our rooms and conjecturing that we were doing this, so we could run away during dinnertime. He was good about it but told us we needed to work a little harder to keep the peace. He never reprimanded us and understood the thrill the excitement had given us. When he brought us back, he told us to bow our heads in shame and act like we had been scolded so the staff would think he had reprimanded us.

Day 53

On the 25th of May, we were informed that the Supreme Court of Texas would be making a ruling within a few days. Our hopes were high that we would be freed. Each day thereafter, we were in continual anxiousness to know what the decision of the court would be.

On those hot afternoons, I would spend time in my room with the youngest boys playing with blocks and doing their kindergarten. I worked hard with Seth, trying to teach him reading before he would finally settle down and do it. William and Samuel were more interested and would quickly get their schoolwork done.

Max Jessop, the son of Rich Jessop, was brought from a shelter in Abilene to Boys Ranch. Mark Strother and Terry Cooper asked if we would take more boys, and we told them we would be glad to. They told me eight more boys would be coming, and we began prepping for them. This, however, was canceled because CPS decided to wait for the Supreme Court's decision.

Chapter Eighteen

We Get to Go Home!

Day 57

O n Thursday, the 29th, we were told that the Supreme Court of the State of Texas would be making its ruling. The boys continually contacted their attorneys, hoping to get word of the court's decision. We hoped and prayed their ruling would be favorable.

At 4:05 pm, Terry Cooper came cruising up to Hamilton in his van, honking his horn the whole way. He came into the house and told us that the Supreme Court of the state had ruled that we be returned to our parents! We were overjoyed! Everyone was jumping with excitement about going back home. All the boys went running through the houses, gathering up their belongings and packing all their stuff.

We were excited and called our parents on our secret phones. Merril's mother, Maggie, told the news media shortly after that her fifteen-year-old son from Boys Ranch had called her in great excitement immediately after hearing the ruling and told her, "We're free! We get to go home!" Terry Cooper brought us into the office and was reading us the news. He read that part and said, "Uh-oh, this is going to get us in hot water! Someone somehow got to the phones without CPS oversight."

We didn't know what kind of trouble we might get into, but this scared us. We weren't ready for any more problems. The previous day, CPS had seen the camera we had snuck in and told the staff to take it from us. So, we decided to take it and the laptop back to Amarillo. Sam had just finished a visit with his mother and his older brother Luke. We called them and asked if they could take us to Amarillo. They said they could, so we quickly gathered up everything we were taking in some black trash bags. Then, we walked around the ponds with some of the other boys, pretending to gather up trash. When we got to the back of the pond, we two slipped through the fence and ran to the waiting car while the other boys continued around the pond, picking up trash.

Mother Annette got to Amarillo late that night and gave me my first haircut since the raid had started. I was worried the staff would notice the change but decided to take the chance. I never heard anything about it later. Seth Allred and my brother Levi took us back to the ranch at 5:30 am, and we climbed through the window to the smell of breakfast cooking. I was tired after being up all night, but we had a visit that morning, so I had to get all the boys ready on time.

Mother Annette, Mother Monica, Mother Esther, and Mother Shannon all came for a visit that day. Sandra Hansen, our CPS caseworker, was there, and she let all of us visit together in one big room. My older siblings Levi, Maryanne, and Shirley also came, and CPS let them join in the visit. CPS was not happy with the Supreme Court's decision and forbade the mothers from saying anything about the ruling during the visit. Afterwards, Sandra Hansen and Lynn Ditto, CPS workers, decided that I could go with Mother Annette for a few hours that afternoon because I was an adult. CPS had allowed other adults who were still in custody that privilege.

As soon as I left Boys Ranch, I began wishing I had stayed, as I did not know how the boys were doing and felt I needed to be there instead of taking this break. I came back to Boys Ranch at 6:00 pm. I didn't want the car full of people to have to go through security again, so I jumped out before they got to the gate and walked through the trees over to our house. The ranch security was worried I was running away, but the boys told them I had gone straight to the house and was fine. That evening, eight of the older boys secretly slipped out of Boys Ranch, going to Amarillo, and had a nice steak dinner while I stayed and put all the younger boys to bed. I had been up all night the night before and was very tired. We let all the boys stay up and play games outside until 9:00

that night.

On Saturday, Terry Cooper told me that it looked like only twelve of the boys would be going home, and we would probably have to stay another thirty days. The writ of mandamus had not originally been filed by all the mothers. He informed me that it could take more time to release the children of those mothers who had not been part of the original writ of mandamus filing. This was severely disappointing to me; however, I kept my hopes up. Mr. Cooper brought us a list of the twelve boys the state had given him who would be going home. We secretly kept in close contact with our parents, hoping for any word that Judge Walther had come to an agreement with our attorneys that would allow all of us to return home.

Day 58

On the morning of May 30, while we were getting our things packed and ready, Seth was playing on my bed and noticed a cord that went under my sheet. He shouted, "A cord!" And before I could stop him, he pulled up the sheet and exclaimed, "A phone!" So, I had to give him a little lecture about how quiet we had to keep the secret. He understood and did well.

Day 61

On June 2nd, just after 9:00 am, Terry Cooper came into the Hamilton House and told us the Judge Walther had decided that all of us would be allowed to return to our parents starting that day. CPS was still allowed a degree of custody over the children and were going to continue their oversight for the foreseeable future. Mr. Cooper turned to me and said,

"Mr. Jeffs, we couldn't have done it without you!" I silently thanked God for giving me the strength to endure. That day, Jim Taylor, a Boys Ranch staff who had been there from the beginning and was always kind to us, told me if I ever needed a character witness later in life, he was willing to be one for me. He was always respectful to us and was there almost daily from the time we came until we left. Many of the staff gave us their business cards and told us to call them if we ever needed any help.

The rest of that day was spent waiting for our parents to come and get us. They had to go through quite a process of signing papers before CPS would release us. Seth Allred and my sister Shirley, his wife, were there, having brought some of the parents for visits that day. CPS was allowing other adults who were brothers, sisters, or relatives of the children in custody to pick up the children if their parents were able to fax the needed papers and signatures, and they took several of the boys to Amarillo after they were released.

Around 6:00 pm, Shirley came and worked it out with CPS to pick up all of Mother Annette's boys and those she was legal guardian to. Terry Cooper wanted me to stay and help keep order, but CPS said we would all have to go. Helaman, Abraham, Jacob, Joseph, and William were all taken down to headquarters and were ready to go. Terry Cooper came to Hamilton House to get me and all my belongings. I quickly said goodbye to all the boys and got in his car. On the way down there, I pulled out my phone and told him I had kept this all the way through so we could have private contact with our parents. He simply gave me a pleasantly surprised look.

We loaded our belongings into the truck Shirley had brought and were taken to a house in Amarillo. It was so wonderful to be free and among our families again. We had steak for dinner. Most of the other boys who had been released that day were there. The house was full of people, so we slept out on the lawn that night. In the morning, Mother Esther and Mother Monica showed up with several of my sisters, and we were so happy to see each other! Many of my brothers and sisters who had been in other shelters called me for the first time since our separation, and it was marvelously wonderful to hear from them. Such joyful reunions seldom come in one's life, for it is often pain, trial, and separation that unite our hearts in a greater love, gratitude, and appreciation for one another.

I wanted to return to Boys Ranch once more to check on the boys who remained, so I rode in with Louis Jessop, Mother Monica, and my sister Naomie to pick up Nephi. After we arrived, I talked to Terry Cooper and several of the boys while waiting for Mother Monica to complete the paperwork. Most of the boys were being picked up that day.

CPS had pressured many of the mothers to acquire homes off the YFZ ranch, telling them that would hasten reunification with their children. Almost all my siblings' mothers had secured rental homes across the state of Texas. Most were in the greater San Antonio area, but some were in Amarillo and others in the Dallas-Fort Worth metropolitan area.

After returning to Amarillo, my sisters Barbara and Marie climbed in the van, and we headed down to San Antonio. I drove most of the way. We reached Mother Monica's apartment very late at night. The next morning, I arose and had the privilege of greeting many of my younger brothers and sisters. It was a happy and cheerful time for us. We were excited and happy to see each other again. It was wonderful to be back with our parents!

I was able to get my driver's license a few days after we left Boys Ranch. I met Uncle Merril and was happy to see him. He was proud of me for standing strong throughout the raid. Uncle Merril took the role of a father for me, and it felt wonderful to spend time with him again. I had leaned on him for support while at Boys Ranch and called him almost daily for fatherly advice. For the first week after our release, I felt like a thick layer of stress was slowly being peeled from my brain. It was the most liberating mental feeling I had ever felt.

Uncle Merril wanted me to visit Father in the Kingman, AZ jail and tell him about my experiences in the raid. I went to Kingman for a week and attempted to visit Father, but he refused to see me. I never learned his reason for refusing. After this, I returned to the home Mother Annette had rented in San Antonio. I was hired by my cousin, Joshua Jeffs, to work for his eBay store he was setting up in San Antonio shortly afterward.

When CPS returned the children, only a few of the families returned to the YFZ ranch right away. As CPS and the court began nonsuiting the children in July, families began trickling back to the ranch.

One Year and One Month Post Raid, Spring 2009

I lived and worked in the greater San Antonio area for almost a year until my siblings were all non-suited and I was able to quit my job. After we first left Boys Ranch, we would visit the YFZ ranch on most weekends, but were not allowed to move back as a family until all my siblings were non-suited in February 2009. They moved back during that month. I was working for my cousin Joshua and had become an asset to his business. I was able to quit my job about the first of May and move back home. It was a joyous time when I returned to live at the YFZ ranch.

Though I'd never wish the trauma of the raid upon anyone, I'm thankful for the experience I gained from it. I learned the meaning of faith and trust in God. He gave me courage and hope when I could find none elsewhere. I found a love and caring in my heart for all the young boys I helped care for. My love and bond with my siblings increased immensely. And I learned the meaning of responsibility for others. The experience of suddenly trying to be mom and dad for the many boys in my care was a tremendous means of growth for me.

Part 3

Post Raid Years

Chapter Nineteen

School Principal

A fter the raid, the YFZ ranch was never quite the same as before. Many of the men began working in the surrounding towns and cities to pay the massive legal expenses the raid had incurred. FLDS members whom Father had not named to be on the ranch were allowed there for the next year. Several media outlets were allowed access to the ranch. Even Oprah Winfrey came. Life had turned upside down.

When Father learned of Oprah's visit, he sent word from jail to his counselors in the First Presidency to cease all communication with the news media and restrict their entry onto the ranch.

Over time, Father would begin ratcheting up the pressure on the residents of the YFZ ranch to abide his teachings and increased the requirements of the religion. The state of Texas held a Grand Jury and indicted several men, including Father, for sexual assault of a minor. Hearings and court trials became the norm.

In May 2009, I relocated to R17, the name Father had given the YFZ ranch, from San Antonio. I worked on several ongoing construction projects on the ranch. Father sent most of his children into "houses of hiding" in Colorado with their mothers to protect them from any more CPS interference. Only his teenage boys stayed in Texas on the ranch. All my mother's children besides Levi and I were gone.

In September 2009, Merril Jessop, bishop of the YFZ ranch, had me begin teaching school. I did not want to be a teacher, but he and Father insisted I do so. I taught seventh and eighth-grade boys with Valiant Barlow. In the spring of 2010, Uncle Merril assigned me to do concrete landscaping work around our large home. In the summer, I worked in surrounding towns with a small electrical crew.

In late summer of 2010, Father had most of his family return to the ranch and had all the men stop working outside of the ranch. He appointed me to take care of the temple grounds. No one could enter through the temple gates without his permission, even after its desecration by law enforcement during the raid. All damage that had been done when it was broken into was repaired.

Late that year, Father had us begin several large projects, including a 10,000 square foot house near the temple; a 72,000 square foot house for him; an extremely strong watchtower; and a huge amphitheater.

Each person that assisted on Father's new home and the amphitheater had to be named specifically by him to do so. He said those projects were a sacred work. He designated the sites they were built upon as holy ground. The deadlines he imposed were impossible to meet, like when we had built the temple. There was a flurry of activity to continue the "building up of Zion" after the disruption of the 2008 raid. Everyone was certain the "prophet", Warren Jeffs, would soon be delivered from prison by a miracle from God.

I was now 20 years old. When school began in September, Father appointed me to conduct a devotional with the school children each morning. (a 30-to-45-minute religious training) He also appointed me one of the teachers of the eighth-grade boys. By December, he appointed me Principal of the school. Being stuck in a classroom after high school had never been in my life plans. I had sworn in my youth to never teach school. I was active and adventurous. But here I was, the Principal. When I was young, the members of the FLDS church had the freedom to choose their vocation in life, but now it had become normal for Father or the bishop to choose for us.

Our private school on the ranch was named Zion Academy. It consisted of grades one through twelve. Boys and girls were segregated in the fourth grade through high school. The curriculum consisted of religious and secular subjects. Physical Education was prohibited. Any activity outside the classroom was restricted to a quick run around the school or doing work: small work projects for building up the storehouse, digging up cactus and picking rocks. The teachers and assistants were appointed by Father.

I enjoyed the interaction I had with all the school age children at the ranch. I checked on the students in their classrooms daily. Often, they'd have a math drill sheet ready that they wanted to race me on. I was beat only once. The sixth-grade girls had a drill sheet for turning decimals into fractions. They decimated me!

Our students were well taught. When we did achievement tests at school years' end, all our students were well above the national average.

Several of the teachers were unmarried girls my age. We were required to always be very formal and proper toward each other. That didn't keep us from having secret crushes, though.

School was very hectic that year. Father claimed to be cleaning up all evil from R17. He sent hundreds of FLDS members from the ranch to Short Creek. When school began, we had 300 students. By the end of the school year, we only had 100. This caused a lot of upheaval and a constant shuffling of teachers. Father loved to control the minutia of the school, and I was required to report in detail to him weekly. He claimed God was personally guiding all of this. We believed him.

In the beginning of 2011, he forbade all church members from using the internet anymore. Internet had always been severely restricted at the ranch but was allowed at the guardhouse by the main gate and later at the far gate by the county road. Now all members of the church were forbidden to use it at all. He had come to realize that evidence seized during the 2008 raid contained damning evidence against him; evidence that could easily turn the FLDS people from following him, and it was leaking onto the internet. He had bishops of the various communities inform his followers that anyone who looked at any of this evidence would immediately be sent away from the Church and lose their salvation forever.

We were told there were sacred records the state had stolen from the vaults of the Temple and Printing Building which contained records of ordinances and teachings that God had revealed to the Prophet. To learn of them without his appointment would be the same as being taught about God's doings by the devil himself and cause us to leave the church. This was enough to scare all of us from looking at anything online. We were not to read any newspapers, either. Radio and TV had already been banned for years. I always wondered what could be so bad in those records that it would cause me to leave the Church. Even wondering was a bad thing to do.

In the winter of 2011, I went to a jail visit in Big Lake, TX to see Father with my siblings Levi and Lenora. There he told us (in the form of a revelation from God) that there would come a time when apostates would come among us and tell us there were dark sins Father had committed. "You must heed them not," he said, "because I (God) have required him to perform sacred ordinances that the wicked do not understand."

He prophesied that a scourge (a terrible, devastating disease) would soon come upon the people at R17 for their disobedience. He told me I would personally witness this disease come upon that land. He stated that I would catch this sickness and would nearly lose my life. This would happen so all evil people would finally be cleaned off R17.

It never happened.

In February 2011, Father had me take one of his wives to R23, a small community Father had established near Pringle, South Dakota in 2004. Just before I arrived, he called his family living there and told them I should stay until Uncle Isaac brought us a message from him. I spent a week there working with my younger brothers chopping wood for all the families in the small community.

When Uncle Isaac arrived, he told me there were two meetings he would be holding with father's family. At the first one, he played a recording of father giving a revelation, correcting Wendell Nielsen, who had been his first counselor, telling him of his many supposed sins and calling him to repentance. Father had removed Wendell Nielsen from his position in the church a few weeks before, telling him he no longer held Priesthood and was to be sent far away from the FLDS people. At the end of the revelation, Father also corrected himself and told us that Lyle Jeffs, his brother, was now the Prophet. I reckoned this was like the time in 2007 when he stated he wasn't the Prophet anymore, so I didn't allow this to phase me. However, many of the family were stunned and in tears.

When Uncle Isaac gathered us for the second meeting, he read us another "revelation" from Father telling us this was simply a test to see what we would do; that Father was still the Prophet, but he had been taken through a great test by God. I wondered why God would do this to us.

Father tried to reason out how God was only telling the truth, but it didn't add up. However, I set it aside and decided to not overthink it. After this, I returned to R17 and continued teaching school.

We finally finished Father's large home in May of 2011, five months after the deadline. I was now 21 years old. Many workers and families had been sent away because of missing the deadline. There was a tall, white concrete wall around the house. No one in Father's family could live there unless he specifically named them. He claimed God was telling him who was righteous enough to live there. He did not name me to move there, and I continued living in his original home.

Chapter Twenty

Whiplash

A s Father's world destabilized, he destabilized ours. As he realized his crimes would become public, his revelations became increasingly erratic and difficult to understand.

We were taught faith, but made to fear

Taught love, but made to hate

The gospel was simple, but so complicated

Told of our free agency

And the chains were bound tighter.

In July 2011, Father sent me from R17 to R23 for three weeks. I had been there for a few days the previous May, helping the surveyor, Edmund Barlow, lay out a large project. Father said it would be a large storehouse used to store materials for the building of the New Jerusalem in Jackson County, Missouri. This is a city first prophesied of by John the Revelator in the bible, and later by Joseph Smith, founder of the LDS church, that would be built during the Millennium of Peace after the Apocalypse. The site of this storehouse was about six acres and was going to have a tall concrete wall around it. There was a massive amount of dirt work required for this project. My main job was driving a 40-ton dump truck. I loved driving the big equipment.

While there, his court trial in San Angelo, Texas began. Father's indictment and the evidence against him was kept secret from us. He had us form circle prayers and take two-hour shifts with several other elders, (a priesthood office in the LDS church and any breakoff from that church), holding circle prayers every 15 minutes. This consisted of three or more men standing in a circle with one elder leading in prayer. Then we sat in silent prayer until 15 minutes were up. After that, we'd stand up and pray again, with the next elder leading the prayer. After two hours, another group of elders would come in and trade us off. We pled with

God to intervene and deliver Father from prison. There were so few men at R23 that we were in prayer most of the day. The storehouse project ground to a halt.

After Father's trial and conviction, he sent word for me to return to R17 in Texas and prepare for the next school year. His sentencing took place immediately upon my return. The jury gave him a life sentence plus 20 years with the possibility of parole in 2038. He was placed in the Texas prison system. We were not allowed to know what any of the evidence was that had caused his conviction. We thought he was being persecuted. He continued to reassure us that God would deliver him. Only the most faithful people of the church would be allowed to see him when this happened.

The state had taped subpoenas for all 78 of Father's wives on the far gate of the YFZ ranch. When his trial was over, I went out there, brought them all in, and gave them to my sisters. My sisters passed them out to the mothers. We were severely reprimanded for doing this by Uncle Isaac, whom Father had placed in charge of his family.

After Father's placement in the Texas Prison system, the language in Father's revelations changed drastically and became more difficult to understand. A lot of it was word salad. Father sent several letters to us, requiring us to build a brand-new school curriculum with no references to the outside world. Any mention of money was forbidden. He said there would be no money used in the United Order. As Principal, I was placed at the head of this work. This was a monumental task, but we set to work to accomplish it. School always started on September first at R17. The curriculum was far from ready but did our best. Naturally, there was a clash of ideas for the curriculum, and as a staff, we had many disagreements on how to proceed. As reports of our disagreements made their way to Father, he began sending teachers away. After one month, he sent me away to R23 and told me to be a caretaker to several of my younger brothers there. This was the end of being the Principal for me.

I liked being at R23. The pressure to conform perfectly to the rules never seemed as heavy there as it did at R17, but R17 was considered the most holy place to be. Father always referred to it in his revelations as "Temple Land."

After spending five weeks at R23, Father had me return to R17. This time, he named me to live in his New House. He called it the "More Holy Habitation." Within its walls, he had one wing walled off separately. This was his special place. Only select wives from among the family who were named to live in the New House could enter his part. He informed me in a message that this was the beginning of the New Jerusalem. I was to live like I was in the New Jerusalem, ready for Christ's second advent. My work was to continue as caretaker of the temple grounds.

In late December 2011, several of my sisters pulled up the flowers in the New House flower beds and were busy replacing them with new flowers. They felt like the men who had chosen what flowers to plant there initially had bad taste. This offended some of the mothers (Father's wives), who wrote to Father about it. Father was angry and told us we were in great error. He named all the older girls to be sent away to R23 for participating in this. He also sent Levi away because he was the son Father had put in charge of the New House. Levi had given my sisters permission to uproot the flowers.

Father said I could decide whether to stay or go to R23. I had already been sent away twice that year and wanted some stability. I had not been involved in the flower ordeal. Father had given me so many tasks that I was barely getting four hours of sleep each night. I didn't care about the flowers.

At midnight, when everyone being sent away were loading their belongings into a trailer, Mother Ora, one of his more trusted wives, found me. She asked me what my decision was. I told her I was going to stay. She pulled out a paper with a message from Father for me. He said (as if it were God speaking) that I, in my pride would decide to stay. But I must be sent away to repent because I was a strong influence on Levi. I must also repent of my pride. He said even if I had made the decision to go, Mother Ora was still to read me this message so I would know to repent. I was shocked and confused. There was no way to meet his expectations no matter what my choices were.

I wondered what next Father might claim God had revealed to him about me. Did God base His judgements off prejudiced reports from the mothers? Did He tell lies? Or was Father making it all up on his own? I had been taught to never doubt Father's word, so I sought to expel these thoughts from my mind.

We left R17 early the next morning and arrived at R23 late that night. After a few days, Father had me move to the "South House" with Nephi and Matthew, two of my younger brothers. I was to be their caretaker. He gave no reason for separating us from the rest of his family there. Levi and the other boys would come over every night and he would read stories to us. He had obtained several banned story books in an old filing cabinet in the school at R17. We knew everything would be fine as long as no one reported to Father on us. It was nice to read something different than the religious books we read over and over. We looked forward to those evenings and had a fun time together. Sometimes I would cook steak and chicken for everyone while he read. Then we would sit in a circle and fill boxes with wood shavings we carved out of sticks. We used them for lighting the fire in the wood stove each morning.

After a few weeks, Father called us back to R17. I no longer got to live in "More Holy Habitation." (the New House) I was told to live in the "Original Habitation." I continued helping on the construction projects. After three weeks, Father sent me away to R23 again. This time I lived in the South House with several younger brothers. We were separated from the rest of his family again. Father had me go to the "A house" where part of his family was living and do the family classes. These classes consisted of group kneel-down prayer and morning and evening trainings which consisted of reading sermons of former "prophets" of the FLDS church. My younger brothers were forbidden from coming to classes; they had been caught swearing a few times by one of our cousins.

After I had been at R23 for a month, Father called upon us to confess every detail of sin in our lives. He said it was necessary to tell him everything to obtain forgiveness from God. Still trusting he was led by God, I wrote to him every detail of any sin I felt I had ever committed. A week later, he had Uncle Isaac call me and tell me I was a nonmember; meaning I was no longer part of the Church. I was stunned; this was a huge blow to me. I had confessed, so I could be forgiven and retain my church membership. I was to go to Short Creek with my brother

Abraham, who was also a nonmember, and live in one of the recently constructed triplexes for three weeks. Then we were to be rebaptized into the Church. I was to repent of my sins. He said that I "was not of full truth telling order" and must confess in greater detail. If I did so, I would be allowed back into the church.

We were taken to Short Creek by Nathan Musser, one of the men living at R23. John Wayman was the bishop there. We were to check in with Bishop Wayman daily and work at Reliance Electric's shop to earn our food and housing.

The day I was to be rebaptized, Father sent a message through Uncle Isaac. It stated that God had revealed to him that I had held back my full confession and had immorally touched my younger sisters. He required I confess to this if I wanted rebaptism. I knew I had never molested anyone on earth. I desperately wanted to be restored to the Church and go back home to R17. I wrote to him about anything I could think of that I could have possibly done wrong. This consisted of a few times I had given my sisters a quick side hug when I had not seen them for a long period of time. He had gotten it into our heads that even hugs were wrong; the only touch allowed was a brief handshake. I felt like I was slowly being broken. A week later, Father allowed Abraham and I to be rebaptized.

He first sent us to R1 in Mancos, Colorado. There were only four workmen there at that time. R1 is the first place Father had purchased in 2003 when he started the "lands of refuge." It was in a beautiful place up in the mountains. Spring was just beginning, and I loved it there. We had no pressing construction jobs. There was a cow to milk, chickens to feed, and eggs to gather. We put manure on the hayfields and worked on the water ditches. When we first arrived, Russel Johnson was the bishop. After a few days, he was sent away by Father. Joseph Jeffs, Father's brother, was called there and appointed bishop. He was sent away after two weeks. After three weeks, Father had Abraham and I return to R17.

Upon our return, Father appointed Levi and I to be drivers for his family. We were to take whoever he sent away to their newly appointed location. We also brought any of his family he declared worthy back to R17. For the next six months, I spent nearly all my time on the road, moving his family around. At this time, his family consisted of 78 wives, 58 children, and six of his elderly mothers whom we called the "grandmothers." Some members of his family were being moved every week or two.

Life on the road was stressful and always rushed. I did many all-night drives and had little sleep. It was also very expensive, but our money for food and travel was supplied by the church. I always looked for the most scenic routes to take. I often drove through the beautiful mountains of Colorado and saw a lot of new scenery. The only entertainment I had when traveling was recorded music and singing that Father had personally approved of. All of it was composed by members of the church whom he had appointed. If I listened to anything else, I would be risking my membership in the church.

Back at R17, he set a deadline for the watch tower to be completed by late June. Nearly all the men had been sent away for spurious reasons, and we missed the deadline. Our punishment was that all the families had to be removed from the ranch by July 1st. He prophesied we would all soon be driven from R17. Levi was also sent away with several younger brothers to R1.

I was kept very busy over the next few weeks, moving Father's family to R23 and houses of hiding in Colorado. I drove 9,000 miles in ten days. Whenever I had a break from driving, I continued working on the tower.

One day when on the tower, several of us workmen saw my Aunt Melanie working in Uncle Isaac's yard. She was dressed like a man. "What is going on now?" I thought. There were only a few of us men left. We discussed why Aunt Melanie was dressing like a man with her hair cut. (females cutting their hair was forbidden) We concluded that Father must have told her to be in disguise for her "protection."

One Sunday evening I was on the tower alone, taking in the sunset. Uncle Isaac came up the steps, bringing Aunt Melanie with him. When he came to the top, he introduced her to me. He said "Ammon, meet your Uncle Wayne." I was dumbfounded and thought it was all a joke. The next morning, I was sent with a load of fruit to R23. On my return, I brought two of Father's wives back to R17. Before I arrived, my friend Mormon Allred called me and said, "Ammon, Wayne is real." "What do you mean, Wayne is real?" I queried. He told me to come talk to him when I arrived. When I found Mormon, he told me that Wayne was a man. God had told Father that Aunt Melanie was a man, not a woman. When she was born, the doctors weren't entirely sure what gender she was, but had concluded she was a girl. She had been married for approximately 30 years but was unable to have children. I was astonished.

Uncle Wayne started helping us on the tower immediately afterwards. A few days later, Uncle Isaac told me I was to move to R23. I was also to take Uncle Wayne and drop him off at a hotel in Castle Rock, Colorado.

I was supposed to keep his transition secret. I never saw or heard from him (her?) afterwards, and I never knew what to make of this situation.

In August, a week after moving to R23, Father sent me to R1. At this point, I was given no reason for these moves. I always loved being at R1. There were only four unmarried young men living there, and we had a good time. I enjoyed living in the mountains. I kept busy fixing fence and working in the garden. On Sunday afternoons, we'd drive up the mountain or hike into one of the canyons. These were forbidden activities, but we always came up with a reasonable excuse.

By September 1st, Father had me return to R17 with many of his family. I continued doing a lot of travel, moving the family around as he told family members they were nonmembers of the church. Once they were rebaptized, they were moved around to various locations. Each of our lives were now a rollercoaster. "Nonmembers" were shunned by "members" of the Church and had to live apart. Being a nonmember was made miserable. Baptism began to seem like a farce instead of a sacred ordinance.

After a month, I was sent back to R23, where I began teaching school to my younger brothers. Many of the family moved back to R17. Soon afterward, the state of Texas began taking legal action against the YFZ ranch and sought its confiscation, claiming it was contraband and subject to seizure, because of the sexual criminal activity Father had carried out there. Father had most of his family return to R23 when this court case was filed against him. He forbade anyone from fighting this court case. This would lead to us eventually losing the YFZ Ranch in 2014.

In March of 2013, Father had me go to R1 again with his teenage sons. The reason given was that I was trying to direct his family and he must separate me from them. I knew I had not done so but was glad to go to R1.

After only two weeks, Uncle Nephi called and told me to go immediately to Short Creek. I was to check in with the bishop, Lyle Jeffs, my father's brother. As I drove into Short Creek late that night, Lyle called me and told me I was to live in a house with his nonmember sons on "the block." This was the same "Jeffs block" I had grown up on.

After I unloaded my belongings into the house, Lyle came over and read me a message from Father. It stated that I was a nonmember because I had been secretly getting on the internet. He also said I was seeking to direct his family what to do. None of this was true. When Lyle finished reading, he said, "You've been on the internet, right?"

"No, I haven't" I said.

"Don't you dare judge the Prophet. You might have desired to get on the internet. Remember Jerold Williams? He was sent away for 'murder of the unborn.' He became angry and apostatized. Uncle Warren later told us Jerold was judged for desiring the sin; not actually committing it. He would have been allowed back into the church if he hadn't judged the 'prophet' and apostatized. God is judging us like He will in the afterlife now," Lyle said.

I was forbidden to have any contact with my family. Father commanded that I work on a construction crew for an FLDS owned business. This crew was to be perfectly loyal and obedient to the Prophet. Uncle

Lyle had to organize a crew that was good enough to suit Father's requirements, and it took him a week. Meanwhile, I worked with his sons in a small woodshop. At the end of the week, Father sent a message that I should stay and do woodwork. I wrote to Father, telling him I had not been on the internet.

Lyle decided I better fulfill the first directive before working in the woodshop any longer. He sent me out on a framing crew for a week. We went to a job in Sacramento, California. While there, Uncle Nephi called me and read another message from Father. He stated that although I hadn't physically been on the internet, I had desired to do so. God was judging me for this. He said if I ever did so again, I would never be allowed to be part of God's Church. He again forbade any contact with my family and said if I did, God would reveal it to him, and I would be cast off forever. I was only to use my phone to talk to Lyle or Nephi. If I did otherwise, my eternal salvation was at stake.

Uncle Nephi was over Uncle Lyle in the church hierarchy. He had me return to Short Creek immediately. I went to work in the woodshop again and quickly learned the nuances of the trade.

At the end of April 2013, Father had me get rebaptized and return to R1 in Colorado. I was now 23 years old. I was happy to go back to R1 and began to enjoy life again. I walked the water ditch every morning and watered the hay fields. After that, I'd work in the garden with a few of my brothers who had come there around the same time as me. We worked on erecting a woodshop during the afternoons.

After a few weeks, Father sent another message to me, telling me if I had criticized anyone in the Church, I should be a nonmember and return to Short Creek. I told Uncle Nephi I had not done so, and he let me stay. I pled with God to let me have some stability in life before I went crazy from all this whiplash. I was able to stay at R1 for five months without being sent away. This was a great relief to me, and I felt my prayers were answered.

I spent most of my time watering the fields and tending the gardens. I found any excuse I could to check on the canal that started way up the mountain. While up the mountain, I'd find berry bushes and go berry picking. In July 2013, Father had us build a small storage building at R1. He gave us a deadline of one month, which we met.

In September 2013, I was sent back to R17. There were only nine people living there. My job was to keep the abandoned houses in repair. Performing the maintenance on the houses became a full-time job.

Spiders were everywhere and the houses were falling apart. One house was full of stinkbugs. Another one had many wolf spiders. A third had hundreds of daddy-longlegs. I realized they were coming in through the dry sewage system. We had a couple firetrucks there and I had learned how to operate them two years previously, so I got the firetruck and flushed out the sewer system in several places on the ranch.

My brothers Helaman and Raymond were there, and I enjoyed my time with them. We would work in the garden together. Some days we spent picking delicious pomegranates; other days we worked in the sugar beet patch or pulled up morning glories. Without the constant deadlines, life was more free.

Chapter Twenty-One

Nonmember

Weekends were always a dread now. Since Father's incarceration in the Texas Prison system, he had been unable to call like he had in previous years. But our lives had become increasingly unstable. Saturday was "visit day" for Father which meant new messages usually came late Saturday evening. I lived from Saturday to Saturday. Long term thinking was a thing of the past for all of Father's family. If I was a member, I hoped there would be no messages for me. If I made it past Saturday, I knew all would be well the next week. When I was a nonmember, I hoped each Saturday I would get a message announcing my restoral to the Church. This was extremely taxing to our mental and emotional wellbeing.

In mid-October 2013, Uncle Nephi called and read me a message declaring me nonmember. I was to move to Short Creek and work in a woodshop again. The sin I was now accused of was doing evil secretly with my younger siblings, slugging them, and holding threats of violence over them if they dared to tell our parents what evils we had done. It was not true. I wondered what Father's point was in accusing me of falsehood time after time. Was this just another test? Why did God operate like this?

I went to Short Creek and worked in a woodshop for eight long months. Father required that I work alone in my own tiny shop. I was allowed to be next door to the storehouse' woodshop, which was operated by nonmembers for the benefit of the Church. I obtained materials for my work from the storehouse woodshop and built dressers, nightstands, desks, bookshelves, bedframes, sewing tables, and dining tables.

I lived in an apartment at Short Creek with several nonmember boys. Uncle Lyle gave us an old 15 passenger Dodge van so we could go to work at the woodshop each day. We convinced him that we needed exercise, so he gave us permission to drive out on the Arizona strip, the strip of land in Arizona north of the Grand Canyon and find a place to run around. We stretched his permission as far as possible to reduce our monotonous life.

In March of 2014, Uncle Isaac asked me if I felt like I was ready to be restored to membership. I told him I was. A week later, he called me with a message from Father which stated that I could not be restored yet. God had told him I was still able to be tempted.

In May, after I turned 24, Uncle Isaac called and told me I needed to simply acknowledge to Father that I had been violent to my younger siblings, even if I didn't remember doing anything. If I did so, I should be restored soon. I wrote to Father that I acknowledged whatever the word of God was, because God knows everything.

Soon after this, I was sent to a house of hiding in Colorado we called Norway, where I lived for eight months. Rich Allred, husband of my sister Rachel, lived there with several of my nonmember brothers. I was happy to leave Short Creek. We had a small woodshop at Norway, but Rich allowed us to engage in other work activities outside. We gardened, chopped wood, and gathered wild herbs. Rich had a fun personality and cared a lot about us. He was a member of the church but was forbidden from having any contact with his family.

We were told in a message that if we had read anything against the Prophet, we were likely to leave the Church for good. We were to confess if we ever had done this.

I wrote to Father about a time shortly after the raid when I had read a comment to a news article in the Deseret News speaking against him. This comment stated that Father had confessed to committing fornication with his sister. I did not believe this was true, but I wrote it to him because of the commandment he had given us. I told him I had wondered about it but did not believe it was true.

A week later, he sent me a message, strongly rebuking me for allowing even a wonderment to enter my mind and affect my testimony of him. He said apostates always lie about the Prophet. He never denied the allegation. I was shocked at his response. I felt sure he would simply tell me it was not true.

While I was at "Norway," Uncle Isaac informed me that my sisters Rachel, Rebecca, and Lenora had apostatized from the church. I was shocked and wondered why. I had no communication with them and could not ask. Father soon supplied the answer. He told us they wouldn't stop masturbating. "Self-enlivening," he called it. Because they refused to stop their immoralities, they had left the church. He rebuked his family for even wondering why they had "apostatized."

I was very sad that my sisters had left. I was close to Rachel and Lenora. I had always looked up to them. I knew if I stayed with the church, I could never have anything to do with them again. Father told us to never speak to them again. If we did, we would be cast out forever.

I saw my brother-in-law, Rich Allred, take this very hard. He loved Rachel and adored their children. He earnestly wanted to talk to Rachel, but Father forbade this. Rich considered losing Rachel and her children a great test God was requiring him to go through to see if he would stay faithful to the church and the "prophet," Warren Jeffs.

In January 2015, at 24 years old, I began feeling terribly depressed because I was still a nonmember. I had been so since October of 2013. Father made it miserable to be a nonmember. We were shunned by those who were members. He had us live and work separately from the members and we lived in very restricted conditions. Often, he would require his nonmember family to live alone in isolation.

I wanted to get married and have a family, though Father constantly taught that we could not get married until he came out of prison. It felt like the years were just passing by and I had no control of the direction of my life. I wrote to Father everything I could imagine that I possibly had done in my life that could have been a sin in his eyes. I rewrote every confession I had ever written before. I hoped with all my heart he would allow me to have my membership restored. He constantly told the part of his family who were nonmembers that they had not fully confessed. "This is why God wouldn't let them be part of His church," he stated. Father claimed to be between us and Jesus Christ. Father told us Jesus would only forgive us if we confessed to him (Father) first and obtained his (Father's) forgiveness and atonement for us. He claimed he was constantly atoning for our sins.

In February, after Father received my letters, he sent me back to Short Creek. I was to live alone and work in a small woodshop alone. Uncle Lyle put me in a one-bedroom apartment with a connected, unfinished shop. An eight-foot board fence surrounded the apartment. I finished the shop and insulated, sheet rocked, mudded, painted, and hung the lights on my own. I was proud of my work. As soon as it was complete, I asked for woodworking tools. Lyle took over a month getting me any tools and I had nothing to do. Sometimes I would sit by an ant bed, watching them for hours. Other times I'd pick up ants with a spoon and place them in a glass jar so I could take them to another ant bed. When I dumped them out, they would fight for hours. I hated being treated like a little boy but Father's constant threat of being damned to hell if I did not obey his every word kept me in line.

Uncle Lyle had allowed me to have a vehicle at my apartment, so I could drive to the storehouse woodshop across town and get materials for building furniture. That was the only traveling I was allowed to do. His boys brought meals to me from the Jeffs block. After they were gone, I would sometimes drive up to the Narrows, a slot canyon where a beautiful stream flowed. One day I hiked up the Narrows and climbed to the top of Canaan Mountain. Another day, I drove to the base of Pine Valley Mountain and hiked to the top. Then I made a terrible mistake—I reported to Father what I was doing.

His response was the most terrible rebuke he had ever given me. He called me a wicked, adulterous, immoral man. He stated that God was trying to help me repent, but I was giving Him a hard time. Then he said if I were to leave the Church, I would quickly commit all the sins of murder. He was claiming I would commit fornication, adultery, drug abuse, and be an accessory to miscarriage or abortion. I was forbidden to hike anymore or leave my apartment. Uncle Lyle was to take my vehicle and check on me daily to ensure I was staying in line. I was to have no contact with my family. After Uncle Isaac read me this message twice, I reflected on it for a few moments. I concluded that I would let this roll off me like water off a duck's back. I began realizing that Father wasn't always right. "Maybe he'll rectify this when he comes out of prison," I thought. When I decided that, I felt much better. Lyle checked on me every day for a week. When he discovered I was a responsible adult, he relaxed.

In August of 2015, after six months of living alone, my brothers Helaman and Abraham were sent from the "Norway" house of hiding in Colorado to live with me. We moved to a larger, unfinished two-bedroom apartment with an attached shop in the middle of town.

We finished the apartment and set up a woodshop. In December, we asked Uncle Lyle if we could move across town to a larger woodshop. He allowed this, and we finished another apartment inside of that shop.

In February of 2016, the FBI conducted a raid in Short Creek. This raid was based on allegations of food stamp and welfare fraud. Uncle Lyle was put in jail, and our access to him was limited. Abraham returned to "Norway" to live with Rich Allred, while Helaman and I remained in Short Creek. Father had us move over to the block where Uncle Lyle's family lived. About twenty members of Father's family moved from hiding to the South House. (now the Dream Center in current day Short Creek) We were to eat our meals at the South House but were forbidden to speak to any of Father's family.

I was now 25 years old. In June, Uncle Nephi read me a message from Father requiring me to confess that I had molested my younger sisters. He commanded me to cease "self-enlivenment" or my opportunity to ever hold Priesthood would be taken away forever. I wrote to Father that I had confessed everything I had ever done, and probably a lot of things I hadn't done. Still, I could only confess to giving some of my sisters a quick side hug, which was no sin. I was doing no "self-enlivenment." I felt deeply perplexed, wondering how I could possibly please Father. I was still fully committed to the church and never considered leaving. To leave was to throw away my eternal salvation.

Chapter Twenty-Two

Banished

In June 2016, Uncle Lyle was released from prison. He was kept under house arrest with an electric monitoring system that included an ankle monitor. Father sent word to him to escape arrest. He escaped and came back to Short Creek, where he hid from the FBI. This was possible because most of the people were loyal and considered his prosecution to be religious persecution.

On the evening of July 2nd, 2016, Uncle Lyle's son, Paul, told me I was needed at the woodshop immediately. I drove there with my brother Helaman and went inside. Uncle Lyle was standing there, waiting for me. He instructed me to hand my phone to Helaman and get in his car. He drove to his office and had me come inside. There, he read me a message from Father, stating that I was now an apostate and must be sent far away. I was to have no contact with my family. I was not to move to any state where church members lived. He directed that I move to a north-central state but stay west of the Mississippi River. I was to continue sending monetary donations to the Church. If I did so, I could eventually be reinstated in the church. He forbade me from writing to him and said I could only write to Uncle Lyle. He again forbade me from using internet. Father was not happy that I would not confess to molesting my sisters. I was puzzled why he would want me to admit to something I knew was not true.

Uncle Lyle was directed to give me enough money for two months' living and an old car. I had no credit established yet, so using a credit card was not an option for me. From there, I was to find a job and a place to live. The internet was still forbidden.

I had never applied for a job before outside of any FLDS owned business. All my time and labor had been given to the Church. It was new to be thrust into the outside world, and I was both scared and excited. I drove away from Short Creek in an old Lincoln Town car with 280,000 miles and a host of mechanical issues.

Despite the stress of my situation, I realized I would finally be able to make my own decisions for the first time. I could decide where I drove and what work I did. I knew I needed to act fast before I ran out of funds. I hoped Father would reinstate me in the church soon but knew many men that had been banished had been gone for years.

Over the course of a week, I made my way to Minnesota and started applying for jobs in several woodshops. After staying in hotels for a few days, I realized that would drain my funds quickly. On my second week out, I drove to Warroad, Minnesota, and applied for a job at Marvin Windows. Then I bought a tent and camping goods at a sports store. I made my way to a secluded spot in the forest and set up camp. I couldn't believe how many bugs and mosquitos there were. Out west was nothing like this. Sometimes, during the night, I'd hear animals tromping through the woods. I soon realized that bears and moose lived there.

After two weeks, Marvin Windows accepted my application and gave me a hiring date. I then drove to Roseau, twenty miles distance, and applied for an apartment to rent. The owner of the apartment building asked me where I was living. I told him I was camped in the woods. He was kind and allowed me to immediately move into an apartment. I paid my deposit and first month of rent. Then I went to work. Marvin Windows paid us biweekly, which meant I'd have to work for three weeks before I was paid. By the time I got my first paycheck, I was down to six dollars. My only furniture was a camping chair and an air mattress, but I was happy to have a roof over my head. No one in my family had any idea where I was.

In October, I found a part-time job offer in the local paper. I contacted the business owner, who sent me to talk to his dad. John Harren met me in a small woodshop he had built for his business, Northern Toboggan Company. John had just turned his business over to his sons, Jack and Gabriel, but he was still the craftsman doing the work. John felt good about hiring me. He also offered to rent me a furnished apartment on his property. I gladly accepted and moved there a week later. I worked at Marvin Windows from 5:30 am to 2:00 pm; then, I drove to John Harren's place and worked in the toboggan shop from 3 pm to 6:30 pm. I loved working with John. He gave me good, practical advice. I knew he really cared about me, and this gave me hope. When I felt depressed about being banished, I'd go spend time with him. I learned there were good, honest people in the outside world.

After living in Minnesota for nine months, I got a call at Marvin Windows from Russel Johnson. Father had sent Russel away "forever" in 2012 but had recently called him back to Short Creek. Russel had searched me out and finally found me. He informed me that Father had invited me to come to meetings that were being held in Short Creek. He told me everyone in Short Creek were nonmembers, but only those Father had named were to attend these meetings.

I left Minnesota immediately to make it to the meeting that weekend. In one of the revelations that were read that Sunday, Father said we would be cast out again if we didn't attend the weekly meetings. I realized I'd have to quit my job and move closer if I wanted to attend. I talked to Russel after meeting, and he suggested I find a job in Utah. In our conversation, Russel told me he expected Father to send him away in a few weeks, because Father had previously sent away the other men he had appointed to conduct the meetings. I drove back to Minnesota and handed in my resignation to Marvin Windows and Northern Toboggan. Then, I drove back to Utah to help my brother Levi who was working on setting up a new business with our cousin, Wendell Jeffs.

Two weeks later, Russel Johnson called me with another message from Father. He told me I was being sent away again with my younger brother Jacob, who was age 19. I was low on money, having donated all I could to the Church. I knew I had to act fast. I gathered Jacob up and headed for Columbus, Nebraska. Before arriving, I contacted Cornhusker Irrigation and applied for a job. They immediately accepted and let us start work right away. We could not find housing, so we moved into the cheapest motel we could find. It cost us $27 a night. It was livable at best. We had nowhere to cook meals, so we lived off cold cereal and processed food. After four weeks, Russel Johnson called again and told us we were invited back to the meetings. Father told Jacob to find a Church affiliated company to work for but gave me no instructions. I was still very devoted to the FLDS church and believed God was allowing me to be tested to purify me. I knew by now that Father didn't always get everything right, but I looked beyond him to a just God who I believed would eventually make everything right in the church. This kind of upheaval was incredibly taxing to my mind. I knew I couldn't survive if Father kept banishing me, then bring me back, and banish me again. I sometimes wondered if Father was trying to break me. I determined that I would not allow myself to be broken.

I was glad to be able to choose my own job. I told Cornhusker Irrigation we wouldn't be able to return. Then I asked my cousin Wendell if I could work for him. His new business, Prime Industries LLC, was just starting. It was tough at first, but Levi and I worked hard. We started with contract fencing projects from Home Depot but soon went on to contract post frame buildings. We dropped the fence jobs and the main work Prime Industries contracted from then on became pole barns.

Chapter Twenty-Three

Is Father Crazy?

The weekly meetings for selected nonmembers in Short Creek continued through the summer of 2017. In the revelations Father was having Russel Johnson read to us, we were told that Father was the only man on earth who held the Priesthood. He said he would come out of prison soon and rebaptize all the faithful back into the church.

Father started claiming great judgments and destructions were happening all over the world. He said many wicked people were being lifted away from the earth and taken in death. He even claimed that President Donald Trump had issued a presidential pardon for him but the guards at the prison refused to release him. Everything he said started sounding crazy. I began wondering if he had lost his mind.

I was now 27 years old. In August 2017, my brother Joseph was sent from R23 in South Dakota to work with Levi and me. He told us Father had told his family at R23 that everyone except five million people in the United States had been lifted off this earth to a planet that was hell and were taken in death. Father said angels from heaven were working in the power plants and any critical infrastructure to keep the nation functioning properly. He claimed the government and news media were keeping this all a secret. I asked Joseph if he was sure he heard Father's revelations correctly. He insisted he had. I concluded that Father was out of his mind. I thought if I waited it out, he would come to his senses and correct the error. I still believed Father was innocent and was held in prison because of the persecution of the wicked.

That August, Father stopped the weekly meetings for a short time. He then reinvited a select few to come and listen to his revelations. I was not among that number. Those who attended quickly distanced themselves from Levi and me. We did not know why. At first, I was worried that Father was again falsely accusing me. But I soon decided it didn't matter anymore. God knew the truth and I was willing to trust Him in the day of judgement. By now, I had concluded that I was not converted to Father. Instead, I was converted to my Savior, Jesus Christ and was willing to trust my salvation with Him.

Levi and I worked for Wendell's business, Prime Industries, for the next four- and one-half years. I acquired new skills and became a proficient crew foreman in erecting post frame Morton Buildings. Our work required much travel. We erected buildings in Utah, Colorado, Idaho, Montana, and Wyoming.

I badly wanted to get married and have a family. I had wanted to get married since I was 18 years old. I had been taught this was essential for my salvation. From my youth, I had been taught that only the Prophet could choose who I would marry. He would have to perform the ceremony. If we married without the Prophet's guidance, it was considered adultery. We wouldn't be allowed into heaven to live with Jesus when we died. If we had any intimate relations with the opposite sex, we were lost forever. Father had emphasized this over and over, especially since he had gone to prison. Back in 2010, he went so far as to forbid husbands and wives from having marital relations. At first, it was only for those at the "places of refuge," but was applied to all the church membership by the end of 2011. By the beginning of 2012, even hugging was completely suppressed for all church members. Father claimed God wanted to teach us the right way to have affection and relations in marriage but was withholding this blessing until Father could be delivered from prison.

I often felt lonely and depressed. I began to spend any spare time I had hiking deep into the mountains and fishing in secluded lakes. Father had forbidden me from doing this once, but now I felt it justifiable. I didn't believe it was wrong. I loved the beauty and peace I felt way out there amid God's most beautiful creations. It was much better than sitting on the couch reading scriptures and religious books. I felt closer to God out there.

In January of 2019, my sister Rachel somehow obtained my phone number. She sent me a text message. The opening words said, "Father sexually abused me when I was young." She did this, knowing I probably would not read her message. I remembered Father teaching us that apostates always lie just to make you leave the Church. I deleted the message without even reading any more of it. I asked my oldest sisters Maryanne and Sandra if any of this could be true. They informed me that Father had never treated any of his daughters improperly. I was satisfied with that and memory-holed what Rachel had said.

In September of 2019, some family members that Father had sent to North Dakota begged me to sign on a house with them. It was near the town of Durbin. They had been renting for two years and wanted their own house. They did not have enough credit needed to buy it on their own, so I finally consented to help. When I came there for the signing, they treated me strangely and accused me of being an immoral person. I realized Father had continued his false accusations against me, and most of them believed him. I still wanted to help them out, so I cosigned on the house, believing this would blow over soon. I was dead wrong.

In December 2019, Father told all my brothers who were working for Prime Industries, the business owned by my cousin Wendell Jeffs, to quit and have no contact with Levi or me. He started gathering many family members to North Dakota. I contacted my brother Joseph, who had returned to R23, and asked him why I couldn't get a message from Father. Everyone else in the family that were asking were getting messages from him and moving to North Dakota. Joseph went to my sister Josephine, who was now one of Father's scribes, and asked her if Father had given any direction for me. She told him Father said Levi and I were supposed to move to Wisconsin but had told her not to tell us. I told Joseph that was not sufficient to make me move. I wanted to hear directly from Josephine. Josephine asked Father again, and he told her that he had already come and told Levi and me in person. She was forbidden to speak to us. Joseph told me Father now added that we were to live alone and repent. I told Joseph this was unacceptable. I would not move to Wisconsin. He became angry with me and told me Father had said Levi and I were apostates. Father forbade his family to have any more communication with us. Joseph refused to speak to me for a long time afterward.

When all my brothers besides Levi had quit Prime Industries, it put the business in a tight spot, and it was unable to do payroll regularly for a few months. Father had everyone move away from the house I had signed on and told them to let the mortgage go. He told them, "Move away from the house you seem to have purchased and rent a house until I come." The mortgage payment for the house in Durbin, ND was put squarely on me, but I was unable to pay, so it went into foreclosure.

In 2018, my work with Prime Industries began bringing me to Star Valley, Wyoming. I loved the region and began working there most of the year. We stayed in rented homes near Thayne most of the time. In 2021, Levi and I purchased a house near Afton, a small town in Star Valley. I was unable to sign with him on the mortgage because of the previous mortgage I was on that was foreclosing in North Dakota. This Star Valley home with Levi was the first permanence I had felt in a decade. It felt so good. Our work still took us to Colorado and Utah, so we decided to start our own businesses and live in Wyoming full-time. In January 2022, we officially moved to Star Valley.

I was now 31 years old. In July of 2021, six of my sisters in North Dakota suddenly left the Church, including Mother's two youngest daughters, Josephine and Amber. I knew they had been in close contact with Father. I wondered what was going on to make them suddenly "apostatize." My older sister Emily came to visit us against Father's wishes. Her two oldest sons had been separated from her for years and were now with Levi and me. She wanted to reconnect with them despite Father telling her they were wicked, and she must let them go. I asked her what on earth was going on with my sisters. Why did so many suddenly leave? I knew they had lost R23 in South Dakota and had all moved to North Dakota. I intimated to her that I knew Father had started saying things that made no sense.

She informed me Father was saying far crazier things than I realized. I asked why they were listening to him at all. She had no answer. She agreed with me that we should not worry about what he was saying anymore and just live our religion where it made sense.

I learned that Father had accused many of us of being on drugs, engaging in prostitution, and murder. He even accused Emily's two youngest children of murder many times while they were very young. Emily knew these were dark lies.

Father had often told us the wicked were seeking his life. In 2007, when he said he wasn't the Prophet, we'd assumed he was being drugged. I suggested perhaps this was the case. Why else would he accuse all of us of being on drugs? She agreed.

In January 2022, members of our family began to treat us fairly again. My brother Helaman stopped by our house in February. He told me one of our "apostate" sisters had informed him that the FBI was giving Father drugs. A week earlier, Joseph had told me the same thing. I knew by this time that Father's family was terrified to do anything that might upset him. If they did, he would falsely accuse them in the name of God of doing the most heinous crimes. I knew none of them would do anything to defend Father, even if they thought the FBI was drugging him to make him say these terrible things. They feared Father correcting them more than they cared for his well-being.

I wrote directly to Father several times, telling him what Helaman and Joseph said about him being drugged. I received no response. When I was younger, Father always told us, "God and the prophet only do right." I told my siblings, "Maybe God and the Prophet only do right, but if God isn't involved in what the Prophet is doing or saying, the Prophet can do something wrong. We must know if God is truly speaking to him." Only a few agreed.

In early April 2022, I communicated with the governor's office in the state of Texas, requesting that this allegation of Father being given drugs by the FBI be investigated. I told the governor that Father was saying crazy things, and his family was trying to believe everything he said no matter how crazy it was. They believed God was still speaking through him. They thought this was just another test of their faithfulness to Father.

I heard nothing from the governor's office for a few weeks. Soon enough, the repercussions came. Father called his scribes in North Dakota and informed them I had contacted the prison, accusing him of being on drugs and saying crazy things. He had Helaman read me a message from him. He told me that in writing these things to the prison, I was turning traitor to God and the Priesthood. He said he never took any drugs, not even simple medications. He told me I could ask his mother, his sister Rachel, and my sisters Josephine and Hannah if he was mentally stable. He was sure they would tell me he was. Then he turned it back on me. He accused me of being on hallucinogenic drugs. He said I was engaging in prostitution with wicked women. He called me to repentance and said this was why I wasn't married yet. Levi and I should now confess these things to him if we wanted to be restored to the Church and have families of our own. He went on to tell the family in North Dakota that we were guilty of many murders. He said I would not hear from him again unless I was rebaptized into the FLDS church.

The next day, I received a letter from the governor's office informing me they had requested Father's medical records from the prison for me, but he had refused them. The letter told me my concerns had been sent to the Ombudsman of the Texas Department of Criminal Justice. The office of the Ombudsman is for providing the public or inmates a confidential avenue for complaint regarding non-criminal matters within the Texas Prison system. That's how my communication had made it into Father's hands.

I did not care what Father said anymore. I knew it was all lies. I sent him a letter the next day, telling him I forgave him for these false accusations. I told him when we met at the bar of God, I would be able to look him in the eye and tell him his accusations were not true. When he received my letter, he informed his family (the select few he named to listen to his calls) that I was now accusing him of lying. He said, "Ammon said he is going to call me before the bar of God. Can you believe that??"

In early May 2022, Helaman called me and read me another message from Father. It told Levi and I to move to a far eastern state and leave Wyoming. We were to have no contact with any members of our family. I had started a regenerative farming business that spring and had hundreds of chickens on pasture. I knew I couldn't dump everything and leave. I also knew everything Father was saying was based on lies. Levi called me and asked me what I was going to do. I told him I wasn't going anywhere. He agreed with me and decided to stay. We continued as if nothing had happened.

Helaman texted me a few days later, informing me Father had said again that if I wanted to receive any more of his word, I was to move far east. I responded that I would not leave everything and do that. I told him if going on a vacation back east was fulfilling that call, I'd do that, but nothing else. I had not turned away from the church, but I knew Father was not being led by God at this time. I knew God only spoke the truth and could not rectify what Father was saying with that principle. I believed he had been led by God before he went to prison, but it was unclear to me when everything had gone wrong. I hoped a miracle would rectify the situation. I felt I would be sinning if I were to obey his directives. Most of our family turned against us again for the next few months. Overtime, they would eventually communicate with us again and stop by to visit if they were traveling in the area. I stayed busy with my work and enjoyed spending any free time I had hiking, fishing, and hunting in the mountains.

Chapter Twenty-Four

Finding Freedom

S ince 2001, Father often emphasized the evil of communicating or visiting with anyone who left the church. By 2010, such action meant excommunication from the church. Now, he began claiming that many people who had left the church were righteous and had a place in heaven. Nearly all my sisters who had left the church were now considered righteous by him. This justified many members of my family visiting them.

I was close to my younger sister, Millie. We'd both held a special place for each other in our hearts since we were children. In May of 2023, she came from North Dakota and visited with my six sisters, who had left in July 2021 and were living in Utah. I asked her to please come visit us in Wyoming. When she never showed up, I asked what was delaying her. She informed me that she had decided to stay with my sister Amber, Mother's youngest child, for a week. Amber was going to have a baby and needed someone to help her in her home duties. I remonstrated with Millie against doing this. I reminded her that Father had taught us all our lives that we should not associate with "apostates," let alone stay with them for a week. Although Father had called Levi and I "apostates" from time to time, we were not considered apostates by anyone in our family. Many in the family knew Father made outrageous, untrue claims all the time. Most of them thought it was a test by God. It had become a form of doublethink. Millie told me she was going to be just fine and had no plans on leaving the Church. I told her I trusted her and hoped she'd still come see us before returning to North Dakota.

My sister Emily seemed very troubled about Millie staying with "apostates" for a week. She told me she was going to send Millie a long text message informing her why she should change her plans. I told Emily I had given Millie enough trouble, but she could do whatever she wanted.

The next day, Emily sent her text message to Millie and copied it to me. In there she stated that *"the girls have more deeper reasons to want you to stay there with them than just to help. I personally know what they want you to hear and be exposed to... and it is stuff that will very quickly and effectively destroy your testimony. It's serious enough that I hardly think a lot of our mothers would even be able to hear it and survive......I have personal experiences that give me room to speak that most others cannot understand."*

After reading this, I called Emily and asked her what on earth she was talking about. She refused to say. I asked her if it was something her ex-husband had told her before he was sent away. Father had banished him in 2011 and they had been separated for 12 years. She said no. Then it dawned on me. Rachel's text message from four years ago must have some truth to it.

I asked, "Did Father sexually abuse some of his girls?"

"Yes," she said.

"Did he abuse you?"

"Yes."

"And Rachel?"

"Yes, but Rachel is overexaggerating. It didn't happen nearly as much as she says. It was only a few times."

"Is that how it was for you?"

"Yes. It was only two or three times."

"What years did this happen?"

"Between 1995 and 1998."

I was stunned. Father was guilty of everything he was trying to make me confess to for the last 12 years. It was he who was guilty of molesting my sisters. I was not satisfied. I dug a little deeper.

"What did he do to you?"

"I don't want to say, only that really bad things happened. But he didn't take my virtue."

"I'm an adult," I said, "you can tell me what it was. Did he make you undress and touch your private parts?"

"Yes, and made me touch his."

I could not believe my ears. Emily went on to tell me that he had repented and shown us a great example of repentance by never doing it again.

I felt like the bottom had dropped out from under my world. I had to know the whole truth. I knew Emily had never spoken to Rachel or any other abused sister to find out their story. All she had said about Rachel's experience was her own conjecture.

I realized if Father had really molested his own daughters, he was not the Prophet. By his own teachings, he would not be able to hold Priesthood authority. God wouldn't be so reckless to choose such a wicked man to represent Him and give us His word.

In the meantime, my sister Millie decided to leave the church. She was among those in North Dakota whom Father considered the most faithful, but she had also learned the truth when visiting our "apostate" sisters. Her mother called me one evening, wondering what exactly had caused Millie to leave. I informed her what Emily had told me about being molested by Father. To my surprise, she told me this didn't affect her testimony of him at all. She reasoned with me that for a man to become a god, he must commit sin and almost commit acts that would destroy his chance of salvation for him to understand the trials the children of God go through here on earth. In the FLDS, taking someone's virtue is considered a sin that will keep a person out of heaven. Emily had stated that Father hadn't quite taken her virtue despite molesting her. This reasoning felt dark to me. Justifying child molestation in the name of becoming a god seemed extremely irrational to me. I searched the bible for my answer and found a quotation from Jesus in the book of Mark chapter 9, verse 39: *"And whosoever shall offend one of these little ones that believe in me, it is better for him that a millstone were hanged about his neck, and he were cast into the sea."* This was my answer. Jesus gave no exceptions.

I knew I had to call my sister Rachel. I still had a lot of prejudice against Rachel that Father had built in us over the years. He had stated that she left because of her own sexual immorality and had passed it on to her children. At first, he tried to get her to return. When she refused, he told us she was consigned to the lowest hell and could never repent.

I decided to purchase her book, "Breaking Free," where Rachel tells her story of life in the FLDS and how Father sexually abused her as a child. I wanted to talk to her after reading it to see if her story matched or if she was exaggerating like Emily had stated. She would not know I had read the book. I bought the eBook version on a Saturday and read it in four hours. I was horrified with her experience. It had the ring of truth to it.

After I finished, I emailed her my phone number, requesting her to call.

Late that night, Rachel called. We hadn't spoken in nine years. I was so happy to hear her again! I had looked up to her affectionately until she left the church. Rachel was very happy to hear from me. She sounded intensely relieved that I had finally been able to see through all the confusion and find the truth. She told me she had never regretted leaving. I asked her what Father had done to her. She matched her story perfectly and told me much more than she had written in her book. She gave me encouragement to seek out the truth and told me she was there for me if I ever needed assistance. We talked almost all night.

The next day, I called my sister Lenora. It was wonderful to hear from her again! Lenora had never gone public with her story of Father molesting her. She told me much of what he had done to her as a child. She told me her story of leaving and how much happier she now was. As we spoke, I felt the weight of many years of being unable to please Father falling off my shoulders. I felt like I could start being happy again.

I did my due diligence and learned Father's pattern of molesting young girls went way beyond Rachel, Emily, and Lenora. I discovered his tendency to molest little girls had started in his father's family before he was married. Several of his younger sisters were victims of his abuse. I learned of the crimes he had committed and was teaching his wives in Texas.

Now it all made sense why he "married" little girls. He had married three of my classmates when I was still thirteen. Then he married girls younger than me. He had told us he had gathered them up for their protection and was only doing what God had required of him. When he had married 12 and 13-year-old girls, he made it appear he was protecting them. I had thought he had no sexual relations with them. Now I knew it was for his lust.

I was deeply saddened and heartbroken by the crimes Father had committed. I knew I had to leave the FLDS. I also felt intense relief that I could go forward in life. I had been stuck in an impossible rut for years. I was now 33 and anxious to move on. Now I was becoming free from the mental chains of darkness I'd been subject to all my life.

In June 2023, I began visiting my siblings that had left. I hadn't spoken to many of them in years. It was wonderful to catch up with them! I knew my family that was in the Church would despise and shun me, but I had to make the choice not to mind. All that mattered to me was the truth.

I carried on with my farm and carpentry work in Star Valley, WY. Soon after I left, a girl still part of the FLDS contacted me through my Facebook business account. She had questions about the church and wanted to know the truth. She recognized me from a picture she had seen thirteen years previous. This picture had been taken by the news media at one of Father's court hearings I had attended in 2010. She had a fake name on her account. While I was out doing my evening chores, I told her by text my story of the last few years and what I had learned about Father's crimes. She, too, had felt that something was wrong. Then I convinced her to tell me who she was. Her name was Jennifer Holm. I had first thought it was one of my brothers in North Dakota spying on me, because I had known them to do that to people in the FLDS they were suspicious of. I learned she was one and a half years younger than me and had been waiting all these years to get married, just like me. She had grown up in Short Creek and now lived in Cedar City, UT. We shared pictures of each other and started talking every morning and night over the phone. We wanted to meet but lived seven hours apart. We decided to have our dates in the Provo, Utah area because it was the halfway point between our homes. At our first date, we immediately fell in love and knew we were meant for each other. Although we had lived in the same community, we did not know each other previously. When we met, it felt like we had been close friends all our lives.

One Sunday morning, we met in Provo Canyon, UT for a date. I took her to the Sundance Mountain Resort. We rode the ski lifts to the top of the mountain, very happy to spend time together. When we arrived at the top, I proposed to her in the shadows of Mount Timpanogas.

Jen kept her choice to leave the FLDS very quiet until the day before our wedding, so she could keep her job and apartment. She worked for an FLDS owned company and rented an apartment from her brother who was faithful to the church. We had both been yearning for marriage for years and were overjoyed to find each other so compatible. We felt ready to move forward in life. Both of us had wanted marriage since we were 18 and felt this was a bit belated, but that made our joy only sweeter. On July 29, we were happily married in Provo, Utah.

Every day, I tell her I couldn't have made a better choice. She says the same. I hope it's true. The depression, sadness, and loneliness are gone like an old dream. Every day is bright and happy. God is good. I have no regrets about leaving. Together we can fulfill our dreams; dreams we didn't dare dream to have during our long years in the church. Our dog, Wes, keeps us on our toes. And hopefully, soon, children of our own will be here, too.

The End... or maybe it's just the beginning!

Epilogue

S ince I left the FLDS, many people have asked me where I stand with my faith. My trust in an all-wise, loving, and kind Providence has sustained me in my most difficult times. My belief that God is just and only speaks the truth gave me the courage to disobey Father and eventually leave the FLDS church, which I believe is a cult. At the time of this writing, I haven't joined any organized body of religion. Leaving the FLDS and sorting truth from error is a lot like peeling an onion—there is layer after layer to go through, sorting truth from error. But my faith in God is firm and my trust in the love and atonement of Jesus Christ is sure.

Jennifer and I think the grandest thing in the world will be a small, backcountry homestead where we can farm like Joel Salatin, one of the pioneers in the regenerative farming movement. We want to give back to the land more than we take and make our future homestead a lovely place to raise our family and build up our local community. Jen is an excellent cook and seamstress and loves to sew blankets and pillows. My favorite hobby next to farming is building wooden toboggans, sleds, and snowshoes. Maybe one day, I'll have a nice woodshop to craft in during the long, cold Wyoming winters.

There are good people in the FLDS church that are only in that group today because they don't know the truth and live under so much control. Dealing harshly with them seems to drive them back into the faith, causes more secrecy, and creates an environment for more crimes to happen. They have been taught for many years that everyone in the outside world is lying about the prophet and inventing his crimes, so any opposition is looked upon as persecution.

The movement the FLDS church sprang from was begun by men who believed they could question changes the leaders of the LDS church were implementing in the LDS church. People from that movement banded together and the group slowly morphed into a religion where no member could question anything that the "prophet" taught or directed. By the time Father was put into prison, the religion was all about him. We arose in the morning on time to please him. He was first in our prayers each day. We obeyed him because we thought he spoke for God. We believed he acted in the place of God to us. Our blind faith in him became our greatest obstacle from learning the truth. Fear became our motivating factor in our obedience to his every word. And we were raised this way from childhood. I hope my story will leave my readers with hope and empathy for others who are caught in like circumstances.

I wrote this book to tell the story of the boys, and to give hope to those still in the FLDS yearning for freedom and happiness; you can leave and still be a good, honest person that makes wholesome life choices. I have never regretted leaving for one moment. I also wrote this book to show how damaging blind faith and obedience can be, especially when motivated by fear to live and behave in certain ways. And to give hope to anyone out there struggling; you can become a survivor! Difficult experiences help us understand and empathize with others who are suffering. It gives us courage to lend them a helping hand. Rising above our challenges and winning is something everyone can do.

Good Timber

The tree that never had to fight

For sun and sky and air and light,

But stood out in the open plain

And always got its share of rain,

Never became a forest king

But lived and died a scrubby thing.

The man who never had to toil

To gain and farm his patch of soil,

Who never had to win his share

Of sun and sky and light and air,

Never became a manly man

But lived and died as he began.

Good timber does not grow with ease,

The stronger wind, the stronger trees,

The further sky, the greater length,

The more the storm, the more the strength.

By sun and cold, by rain and snow,

In trees and men good timbers grow.

Where thickest lies the forest growth

We find the patriarchs of both.

And they hold counsel with the stars

Whose broken branches show the scars

Of many winds and much of strife.

This is the common law of life.

— Douglas Malloch

Glossary of Terms

FLDS:

Fundamentalist Church of Jesus Christ of Latter-Day Saints

Short Creek:

Twin Cities of Colorado City, AZ and Hildale, UT

R1:

First "Place of Refuge" established by Warren Jeffs near Mancos, Colorado. Approximately 180 acres.

R17:

Second "Place of Refuge" established by Warren Jeffs. The Yearning For Zion Ranch near Eldorado, TX. Approximately 1700 acres.

R23:

Third "Place of Refuge" established by Warren Jeffs near Pringle, SD. Approximately 145 acres

CPS:

Child Protective Services

BCFS:

Baptist Child and Family Services

CASA:

Court Appointed Special Advocate

MHMR:

Mental Health, Mental Retardation. Sometimes called My Health My Resources

DPS:

Texas Department of Public Safety

Texas Rangers:

A Division of the Texas Department of Public Safety

United Order:

An organization within the FLDS Church where members have "all things in common."

Acknowledgements

I want to express my gratitude to the following people:

Dan Adams, Mark Strother, Terry Cooper, Jim Taylor, Ted Carver, and all others of the Boys Ranch staff who helped keep us encouraged while we were detained at Cal Farley's Boys Ranch.

John and Patricia Harren, for giving me hope and love while banished from home.

My sisters Rachel, Lenora, Josephine, Amber, and Millie for encouraging me to write this book, giving me tips, and assisting in the copyediting.

My wife Jennifer, for her constant love and support. And proofreading.

Tiffany Avery, my developmental editor for the incredible insight she gave.

Stephanie Henderson, a friend, for assisting in the editing and giving crucial insight.

Mark and Linda Hunter, for being true friends and giving me hope and courage when I was leaving.

About the author

Ammon Jeffs grew up in the Fundamentalist Church of Jesus Christ of Latter-Day Saints, which he left in 2023. He lives with his wife Jen, his dog Wes, a herd of sheep, and a flock of chickens in Wyoming. He enjoys hiking, hunting, and fishing. Building toboggans, a trade he learned from his mentor, John Harren, is one of his favorite hobbies.